ANTHOLOGY OF BAROQUE MUSIC

The Norton Introduction to Music History

Anthology of
BAROQUE MUSIC

Music in Western Europe, 1580–1750

Edited by JOHN WALTER HILL

University of Illinois, Urbana-Champaign

W·W·NORTON & COMPANY   New York · London

W. W. Norton & Company has been independent since its founding in 1923, when William Warder Norton and Mary D. Herter Norton first published lectures delivered at the People's Institute, the adult education division of New York City's Cooper Union. The Nortons soon expanded their program beyond the Institute, publishing books by celebrated academics from America and abroad. By mid-century, the two major pillars of Norton's publishing program—trade books and college texts—were firmly established. In the 1950s, the Norton family transferred control of the company to its employees, and today—with a staff of four hundred and a comparable number of trade, college, and professional titles published each year—W. W. Norton & Company stands as the largest and oldest publishing house owned wholly by its employees.

Designed by Jo Anne Metsch.
The text of this book is composed in Bembo.
Composition by TSI Graphics.

Manufacturing by Quebecor World—Eusey Division.
Production manager: Ben Reynolds.

ISBN 0-393-97801-X (paperback)

W. W. Norton & Company, Inc., 500 Fifth Avenue, New York, N.Y. 10110–0017
www.wwnorton.com
W. W. Norton & Company Ltd., Castle House, 75/76 Wells Street, London W1T 3QT

1 2 3 4 5 6 7 8 9 0

CONTENTS

CONTENTS

vi

PREFACE

This anthology serves as a companion to *Baroque Music* in the Norton Introduction to Music History series. All of the works included here are discussed in that book. The selection of pieces for inclusion was guided, above all, by the objective of the book: to provide a balanced survey of the period. This anthology is supplemented by a collection of forty-four additional scores accessible online through the Web site of W. W. Norton & Company at www.wwnorton.com/college/music/Hill. Most of the works in this anthology and in the Web-based supplement are available in good, recent recordings. Many of those that are not have been recorded by students at the School of Music of the University of Illinois, Urbana-Champaign, or, in the case of several works for harpsichord or organ, they have been recorded with synthesized sound via MIDI files. These non-commercial recordings are available on a Web site maintained by the author and accessible via his personal page through the Web site of the University of Illinois School of Music.

The pieces and excepts in this anthology appear in new scores, created with the invaluable help of research assistants at the University of Illinois, Urbana-Champaign: Gregory Hellenbrand, Sharon Hudson, Sonia Lee, Patrizia Metzler, and Kenneth Smith. While these are not critical editions, the original note values, meter signs, key signatures, text spelling, and instrument names have been retained from the printed or manuscript source cited. The original clefs are indicated by small annotations above the modern clef signs at the beginning of each piece. Thus, G2 means treble clef (G on line 2), F4 means bass clef (F on line 4), C1 means soprano clef (C on line 1), and so on. Translations of non-English texts run above the vocal staves. In addition, texts and translations formatted as poetry are included after each vocal score.

Because some errors are inevitable when transcribing so much music, we ask that readers who find mistakes in these scores write to W. W. Norton so that corrections may be incorporated in subsequent printings.

A period source for each work is briefly noted in its heading. Manuscript sources are cited by library and shelf number. The following abbreviations are used to identify these libraries:

A:Wn = Österreichische Nationalbibliothek, Musiksammlung, Vienna
CZ:KR = Knihovna Arcibiskupskéko Zámku, Kroměřiž

D:Bk = Staatliche Museen Preussischer Kulturbesitz, Kunstbibliothek, Berlin
D:Bsb = Staatsbibliothek zu Berlin Preussicher Kulturbesitz, Berlin
D:Kl = Gesamthochschul-Bibliothek, Landesbibliothek und Murhadsche Bibliothek, Musiksammlung, Kassel
D:LEm = Leipziger Stadtische Bibliotheken, Musikbibliothek, Leipzig
D:Mbs = Bayerische Staatsbibliothek, Munich
E:LPA = Catedral de Canarias, Las Palmas de Gran Canaria
F:Pn = Bibliothèque Nationale de France, Paris
F:V = Bibliothèque Municipale, Versailles
F:TOm = Bibliothèque Municipale, Tours
GB:Cfm = Fitzwilliam Museum, Department of Manuscripts and Printed Books, Cambridge
GB:Cu = University Library, Cambridge
GB:Lam = Royal Academy of Music Library, London
GB:Lbl = British Library, London
GB:Ob = Bodleian Library, Oxford
GB:Och = Christ Church Library, Oxford
GB:T = St. Michael's College Library, Tenbury Wells (on deposit at GB:Ob)
I:Bc = Civico Museo Bibliografico Musicale, Bologna
I:Bsb = Basilica di S. Petronio, Archivio Musicale, Bologna
I:MOe = Biblioteca Estense e Universitaria, Modena
I:Pu = Biblioteca Universitaria, Padua
I:Rc = Biblioteca Casanatense, sezione Musica, Rome
I:Rvat = Biblioteca Apostolica Vaticana, Rome
I:Tn = Biblioteca Nazionale Universitaria, sezione Musicale, Turin
I:Vc = Conservatorio di Musica Benedetto Marcello, Biblioteca, Venice
I:Vmn = Biblioteca Nazonale Marciana, Venice
MEX:Pc = Catedral Metropolitana, Archivo del Cabildo, Puebla
S:Uu = Universitetsbiblioteket, Uppsala
US:SFsc = San Francisco State University, Frank V. de Bellis Collection, San Francisco

JOHN WALTER HILL
May 2004

ANTHOLOGY OF BAROQUE MUSIC

1 JACOPO PERI, *L'Euridice* (1600), Prologue and excerpt from Scene 2

from *Le musiche di Iacopo Peri nobil fiorentino sopra L'Euridice*

(Florence, 1600)

1 Jacopo Peri, *L'Euridice*, from the printed score (Florence, 1600)

Prologo

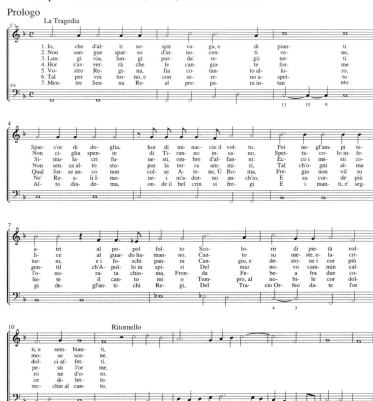

PROLOGO
La Tragedia:

PROLOGUE
Tragedy:

Io che d'alti sospir vaga, e di pianti
Spars'or di doglia hor di minaccie il volto
Fei negl'ampi teatri al popol folto
Scolorir di pietà volti, e sembianti.

I, who, eager for loud sighs and tears,
my face now filled with sorrow, now with threats,
once made the faces of the crowd in great theaters
turn pale with pity.

Non sangue sparso d'innocenti vene
Non ciglia spente di Tiranno insano
Spettacolo infelice al guardo humano
Canto su meste, e lacrimose scene.

No longer of blood shed by innocent veins,
nor of eyes put out by the insane tyrant,
unhappy spectacle to human sight,
do I sing now on this gloomy and tear-filled stage.

Lungi via lungi pur da regii tetti
Simulacri funesti, ombre d'affanni
Ecco i mesti coturni, e i foschi panni
Cangio, e desto ne i cor più dolci affetti.

Away, away from this royal house,
funereal images, shades of sorrow!
Behold, I change my gloomy buskins and dark robes
to awaken in the heart sweeter emotions.

Hor s'avverrà, che le cangiate forme
Non senza alto stupor la terra ammiri
Tal ch'ogni alma gentil ch'Apollo inspiri
Del mio novo cammin calpesti l'orme.

Should it now come to pass that the world admire,
with great amazement, these changed forms,
so that every gentle spirit that Apollo inspires
will tread in the tracks of my new path.

Vostro Regina sia cotanto alloro
Qual forse anco non colse Atene, ò Roma
Fregio non vil su l'onorata chioma
Fronda Febea fra due corone d'oro.

Yours, Queen, will be so much laurel,
that perhaps not even Athens or Rome gathered more,
an ornament worthy of those honored tresses,
a frond of Phoebus between two crowns of gold.

Tal per voi torno, e con sereno aspetto
Ne Reali Imenei m'adorno anch'io
E sù corde più liete il canto mio
Tempro al nobile cor dolce diletto.

Thus changed, I return; serenely,
I, too, adorn myself for the royal wedding,
and temper my song with happier notes,
sweet delight to the noble heart.

Mentre Senna Real prepara intanto
Alto diadema, onde il bel crin si fregi
E i manti, e seggi degl'antichi Regi
Del Tracio Orfeo date l'orecchie al canto.

While the royal Seine prepares
a noble crown to decorate the beautiful hair,
and the mantle and throne of the ancient kings,
listen to the singing of Orpheus of Thrace.

Scene 2, excerpt

Dafne ritorna in Scena Sola. *Dafne returns to the stage alone.*

2

226 *has taken you from me,   who has taken you from me, alas!   Where have you gone?   Soon you will see that not in vain*

mi t'ha tol- to,   Chi mi t'ha tol- to, ohi- me! do- ve sei gi- ta?   To- sto ve- drai   ch'in va- no

235 *did you call, while dying, your husband.   I am not, am not far away.   I am coming, dear life,   o dear death.*

Non chia- ma- sti mo- ren- do il tuo con- sor- te   Non son, non son lon- ta- no: Io ven- go, o ca- ra vi- ta, o ca- ra mor- te.

Dafne ritorna in Scena Sola.	*Dafne returns to the stage alone.*

Dafne:
Lassa! che di spavento e di pietate
Gelami il cor nel seno!
Miserabil beltate
Com'in un punto, ohimè! venisti meno.
Ahi! che lampo, o baleno
In notturno seren ben ratto fugge
Ma più rapida l'ale
Afretta humana vita al di fatale.

Dafne:
Alas! What terror and what pity
freeze my heart within my breast!
Miserable beauty,
how is it, alas, that you faded away?
Ah! As in a flash of lightning,
at night, the calm disappears,
but even more rapidly
human life hurries its flight toward the day of death.

Arcetro:
Oimè! che fia giamai?
Pur or tutta gioiosa
Al fonte degl'allor costei lasciai.

Arcetro:
Alas! What has happened?
But a moment ago all full of joy
I left her near the brook of laurels.

Dafne:
O giorno pien d'angoscia, e pien di guai.

Dafne:
O day filled with anguish and filled with woe!

Orfeo:
Qual così ria novella
Turba il tuo bel sembiante
In così lieto di, gentil donzella?

Orfeo:
What bad news
disturbs your beautiful face,
on this happy day, gentle maiden?

Dafne:
O del gran Febo, e delle sacre Dive
Pregio sovran', di queste selve onore,
Non chieder la cagion del mio dolore.

Dafne:
O worthy sovereign of great Phoebus and of the
sacred muses, honored of these woods,
do not ask the reason for my sorrow.

Orfeo:
Ninfa, deh sia contenta
Ridir perchè t'affanni
Che taciuto martir troppo tormenta.

Orfeo:
Nymph, be pleased
to tell us why you are troubled
for, silent, the martyr torments us too much.

Dafne:
Com'esser può giamai
Ch'io narri, e ch'io riveli
Si miserabil caso? Ò fato, ò Cieli!
Deh lasciami tacer troppo il saprai.

Dafne:
How can I ever
explain and reveal
such an unhappy event? O fate, o heavens!
Ah, let me be silent, for you will know too much.

Arcetro:
Di'pur: sovente del timor l'affanno
È de l'istesso mal men grave assai.

Arcetro:
Tell us: often the fear of sorrow
is worse than knowing the truth.

Dafne:
Troppo più del timor sia grave il danno.

Orfeo:
Ah! non sospender più l'alma turbata.

Dafne:
Per quel vago boschetto
Ove rigando i fiori
Lento trascorre il fonte degl'allori
Prendea dolce diletto
Con le compagne sue la bella sposa
Chi violetta, o rosa
Per far ghirland'al crine
Togliea dal prato, o dall'acute spine
E qual posand'il fianco
Su la fiorita sponda
Dolce cantava, al mormorar dell'onda;
Ma la bella Euridice
Movea danzando il piè sul verde prato
Quand'ahi ria sorte acerba!
Angue crudo, e spietato
Che celato giacea tra fiori, e l'erba
Punsele il piè con si maligno dente
Ch'impalidì repente
Come raggio di Sol che nube adombri
E dal profondo core con un sospir mortale
Si spaventoso ohimè sospinse fuore
Che quasi havesse l'ale
Giunse ogni Ninfa al doloroso suono
Et ella in abbandono
Tutta lasciosi all'or nell'altrui braccia.
Spargea il bel volto, e le dorate chiome
Un sudor viè più fredd'assai che giaccio
Indi s'udio'l tuo nome
Tra le labbra sonar fredd'e tremanti
E volti gl'occhi al cielo
Scolorito il bel volto, e bei sembianti
Restò tanta bellezza immobil gielo.

Arcetro:
Che narri, ohimè, che sento?
Misera Ninfa, e più misero amante,
Spettacol di miseria e di tormento!

Dafne:
The catastrophe is much more serious than the fear of it.

Orfeo:
Ah! Do not keep in suspense the troubled soul.

Dafne:
In that beautiful little woods,
where, bordered by flowers,
slowly flowed the brook of laurels,
she took sweet delight
with her companions, the beautiful bride,
who picked violets and roses
to make garlands for her hair
from the meadow and from among the sharp thorns.
And while bending over
the flowering banks,
she sang sweetly to the murmuring of the stream.
But the beautiful Euridice
danced gracefully across the green meadow,
when, o bitter, evil fate,
a cruel and implacable snake,
who lay concealed among the flowers and the grass,
bit her foot with such evil teeth,
that she paled suddenly
like the sunlight veiled by clouds,
and from the bottom of her heart came a mortal sigh
so terrifying, alas,
as though they had wings,
every nymph came rushing at that pitiful sound,
and she, nearly senseless,
fell into their arms.
Prom her beautiful face and golden hair
came a sweat colder than ice;
and then your name
was heard to sound from her cold and trembling lips,
and her eyes turned to heaven
her beautiful face without color
so much beauty became a lifeless object.

Arcetro:
What do you tell, alas, what do I hear?
Unhappy nymph, and more unhappy lover,
spectacle of misery and torment!

Orfeo:
Non piango e non sospiro
O mia cara Euridice,
Che sospirar che lacrimar non posso
Cadavero infelice.
Ò mio core, ò mio speme, ò pace ò vita
Oimè! chi mi t'ha tolto
Chi mi t'ha tolto, ohimè! dove sei gita?

Tosto vedrai ch'in vano
Non chiamasti morendo il tuo consorte
Non son, non son lontano
Io vengo, ò cara vita, ò cara morte.

Orfeo:
I do not weep, and I do not sigh,
o my dear Euridice,
for to sigh, to weep, I am unable,
like an unhappy corpse.
Oh my heart, oh my hope, oh peace, oh life!
Alas! Who has taken you from me,
Who had taken you from me, alas! Where have you gone?
Soon you will see that not in vain
did you call, while dying, your husband.
I am not far away.
I am coming, dear life, oh dear death.

2 EMILIO DE' CAVALIERI, *Rappresentatione di anima, et di corpo* (1600), excerpt

from *Rappresentatione di anima, et di corpo . . . per recitar*

cantando (Rome, 1600)

Anima:	Soul:
Via, via, false Sirene	Away, away, false sirens,
Di frodi, e inganni piene:	full of fraud and deceptions:
Il fin del vostro canto	the result of your enchantment
Occupa sempr'il pianto:	is always tears.
Ogni diletto è breve,	Every delight is brief,
ma qual ch'affliggerà, finir non deve.	but that which will afflict one never ends.

3 GIULIO CACCINI, *Deh, dove son fuggiti* (1602)

from his *Le nuove musiche* (Florence, 1602)

Deh, dove son fuggiti,	Ah, to where have they fled?
Deh, dove son spariti	Ah, to where have they disappeared:
Gl'occhi de quali ai rai	the eyes by whose rays
Io son cener omai?	I am burnt to a cinder by now?
Aure, aure divine,	Breezes, divine breezes,
Ch'errate peregrine	which wander
In questa part'e in quella,	here and there:
Deh, recate novella	ah, bring me news
Dell'alma luce loro,	of their sweet light,
Aure, ch'io me ne moro.	breezes, for which I die.

4 GIULIO CACCINI, *Udite, udite amanti* (1602)

from his *Le nuove musiche* (Florence, 1602)

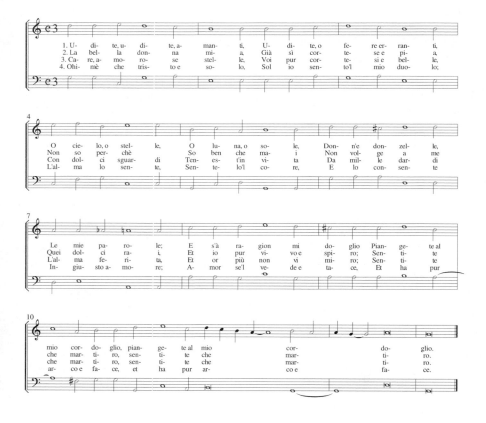

Udite, udite, amanti,
Udite, o fere erranti,
O cielo, o stelle,
O luna, o sole,
Donn'e donzelle,
Le mie parole;
E s'à ragion mi doglio
Piangete al mio cordoglio.

La bella donna mia,
Già si cortese e pia,
Non so perchè
So ben che mai
Non volge a me
Quei dolci rai.
Et io pur vivo e spiro;
Sentite che martiro.

Care, amorose stelle,
Voi pur cortesi e belle
Con dolci sguardi
Tenest'in vita
Da mille dardi
L'alma ferita,
Et or più non vi miro;
Sentite che martiro.

Ohimè che tristo e solo,
Sol io sento'l mio duolo;
L'alma lo sente,
Sentelo'l core,
E lo consente
Ingiusto amore;
Amore se'l vede e tace,
Et ha pur arco e face.

Listen, listen, lovers,
listen, oh wandering beasts,
oh sky, oh stars,
oh moon, oh sun,
ladies and damsels,
to my words.
And if, with reason, I complain,
weep at my sorrow.

My beautiful lady,
once so kind and gentle,
I do not know why,
but I know very well,
looks not upon me
with those sweet eyes.
And yet I live and breathe;
hear what martyrdom is mine.

Dear, loving eyes,
you who are kind and beautiful
with sweet glances,
you keep alive,
although wounded by a thousand arrows,
my soul.
And now I see you again;
hear what martyrdom is mine.

Alas, how sad and alone
I feel my sorrow;
my soul feels it,
my heart feels it,
and it is permitted by
unjust Love.
Love sees it and speaks not,
although he has a bow and a torch.

5 GIULIO CACCINI, *Torna, deh torna, pargoletto mio* (1602)

from his *Le nuove musiche* (Florence, 1602)

Torna, deh torna pargoletto mio
Torna, che senza te son senza core!
Dove t'ascondi, ohimè? Che t'ho fatt'io,
Ch'io non ti veggio e non ti sento, Amore?
Corrimi in braccio omai, spargi d'oblio
Questo, che'l cor mi strugge, aspro dolore.
Senti de la mia voce il flebil suono
Tra pianti e tra sospir chieder perdono.

Come back, oh come back my baby,
come back, for without you I am without heart!
Where are you hiding, alas? What have I done
that I do not see you and do not hear you, love?
Run now to my embrace; cast into forgetfulness
that which destroys my heart, that bitter pain.
Hear the weak sound of my voice,
amidst tears and sighs, begging forgiveness.

6 GIUSEPPINO CENCI, *Io che l'età solea* (ca. 1600)

from I:Vc, Torrefranca 250

Io che l'età solea viver nel fango
Hoggi mutato il cor da quel che soglio
D'ogn'immondo pensier mi purgo spoglio
E'l mio grave fallir correggio e piango.

Di servir falso duce io mi rimango;
A te mi dono ad ogn'altro mi toglio.
Ne rotta nave mai parti da scoglio
Si pentita dal mar com'io rimango.

E poi ch'a mortal rischio e gita in vano
E senza frutto i cari giorni ha spesi
Questa mia vita in porto ho mai t'accolgo.

Reggami per pietà tua santa mano,
Padre del ciel, che poi che a te mi volgo
Tanto t'adorerò quanto t'offesi.

I, who for so long used to live in mud,
today, my heart changed from what I wont,
of every impure thought I purge and divest myself,
and my grave error I correct and repent.

I renounce serving a false leader.
To you I give myself and cut myself off from every other.
Nor did any broken ship escape from the rocks
as wary of the sea as I am.

And since at mortal risk it has voyaged in vain
and without profit spent its weary days,
this life of mine I welcome to port.

Extend to me, for pity's sake, your sacred hand,
heavenly Father, now that I turn to you:
I will adore you as much as I have offended you.

7 SIGISMONDO D'INDIA, *Riede la primavera* (1609)

from his *Le musiche di Sigismondo D'India . . . da cantar solo* (Milan, 1609)

Riede la primavera,	Springtime is laughing,
Torna la bella Clori,	the beautiful Cloris returns,
Odi la rondinella,	the swallow sings,
Mira l'erbette e i fiori.	"Admire the grass and the flowers."
Ma tu, Clori più bella,	But you, fair Cloris,
Ne la stagion novella	in the new season,
Serbi l'antico verno.	you preserve the old winter.
Deh, se hai pur cinto il cor di ghiaccio eterno,	Ah, if your heart is locked in eternal ice,
Perchè, ninfa crudel quanto gentile,	why, cruel nymph but kind,
Porti ne gli occhi il sol, nel volto aprile?	do you wear the sun in your eyes and April in your face?

8 ORAZIO MICHI DELL'ARPA, *Su l'oriente* (ca. 1630)

from I:Rc, MS 2490

*In Greek mythology, Tantalus, a son of Zeus, was condemned to stand in water that receded when he tried to drink.

Su l'oriente
L'alba ridea
Forse perche vedea
Fulminata la notte, e l'ombre spento;
Quando repente
Atra nebbia levossi, e'l sol rapì.
Poi che in fati del dì
Vid'io guardando in giro
Che rapide fuggiro,
Come s'havesser l'ali,
Le vite de' mortali,
E la speme, e'l desio schernito fù,
Folli noi di qua giù;
Rio fugace è'l piacer, ch'al mar sen va;
E per Tantalea sete acqua non ha.

In the east
the dawn laughed,
perhaps because she saw
night being burnt away and the shadows extinguished,
when suddenly
a black cloud arose, and the sun was carried off:
whence, in the events of the day,
I saw, looking about,
how rapidly they flee,
as if they had wings,
the lives of mortals,
and hope and desire were mocked.
Fools we are, here below!
A rushing brook is pleasure that hastens to the sea.
And for the thirst of Tantalus it has no water.

9 LUIGI ROSSI, *Hor che l'oscuro manto* (ca. 1640)

from GB:Och, Mus. M. 946

43

Hor che l'oscuro manto
della notte ricopre il ciel d'intorno,
alla cruda beltà ch'adoro tanto,
fortunato amator, faccio ritorno.

Sù, mio cor, con dolci accenti
fa' che desti i vaghi rai
per cui perdono i tormenti
la crudeltà che non si stanca mai.

Amanti, o voi che siete
pien' di cure e d'affanni,
se trovar non sapete
in un guardo gentil conforto al core,
sempre, sempre a languir con vario stile
vi condanni Amore.

Mentre sanno influir due luci belle
tutto il ben che quaggiù piovon le stelle,
da due nere pupille
io sol chiedo un sguardo,
poi sen vada in favillel'alma trafitta da sì dolce
dardo:
beltà che sia negl'occhi armata e forte
ha saette di vita e non di morte.

Godete, martiri,
trionfi il mio core,
dal regno d'Amore
nessun si ritiri;
quest'alma lo sa:
bellezza, fierezza
in seno non ha.

Hor che Lilla mi rimira
il mio cor più non sospira,
ond'io pur godo se per lei tanto ardo:
a chi si strugge è gran conforto un sguardo.

Now that the dark mantle
of night recovers the sky all around,
to the cruel beauty whom I adore so much,
a fortunate lover, I return.

Come, my heart, with sweet words
awaken those beautiful eyes
for which I pardon the torments
and that cruelty that never tires.

Lovers, oh you who are
full of cares and anxieties,
if you know not how to find,
in a glance, gentle comfort for your heart,
always, always to languish in various ways
does Love condemn you.

While two beautiful eyes know how to gather in
all that is good which rains down from the stars,
from two dark eyes
I ask only a glance,
then my soul may go up in flames wounded by such
a sweet arrow:
such beauty in the eyes, armed and strong,
has arrows of life and not of death.

Rejoice, martyrs!
Let my heart triumph!
From the kingdom of Love
let no one retreat;
my soul knows it:
beauty has no wrath
in its bosom.

Now that Lilla looks at me
my heart no longer sighs,
whence I take pleasure that I burn so much for her:
for one who is destroyed, one glance is a great comfort.

10 CLAUDIO MONTEVERDI, *L'Orfeo* (1607), excerpts

from his *L'Orfeo, favola in musica* (Venice, 1609)

Toccata che si suona avanti il levar de la tela tre volte con tutti li stromenti, e si fa un Tuono più alto volendo sonar le trombe con le sordine.

Toccata, which is played before the raising of the curtain with all the instruments, and it is played a step higher, because the trumpets should be played with mutes.

Act II, messenger scene through Orfeo's lament

PROLOGO

La Musica:
Dal mio Permesso amato a voi ne vengo.
Incliti eroi sangue gentil de Regi,
Di cui narra la Fama eccelsi pregi,
Nè giunge al ver perch'è tropp'alto il segno.

Io la musica son ch'ai dolci accenti
So far tranquillo ogni turbato core
Et hor di nobil'ira et hor d'amore
Poss'infiammar la più gelate menti.

Io su cetera d'or cantando soglio
Mortal orecchio lusingar tal'hora
E in questa guisa a l'armonia sonora
Dela lira del ciel più l'alme invoglio.

Quinci a dirvi d'Orfeo desio mi sprona,
D'Orfeo che trasse al suo cantar le fere

E servo fe' l'Inferno a sue preghiere,
Gloria immortal di Pindo e d'Elicona.

Hor mentre i canti alterno, hor lieti hor mesti
Non si mova augellin fra queste piante,
Ne s'oda in queste rive onda sonante,

Et ogni auretta in suo commin s'arresti.

PROLOGUE

Music:
From my beloved Permessus, to you I come.
Famous heros, noble blood of kings,
of whom Fame recounts their great exploits:
she falls short of the truth concerning them because
the subject is too elevated.

I am Music, who, with sweet accents,
know how to calm every agitated heart;
and now with noble wrath, and now with love,
I can inflame the most frigid intellect.

I, to the sound of my golden lyre, singing,
I long to charm mortal ears
and, in this way, to the resounding harmony
of my heavenly lyre, to transport more souls.

Thus, a desire spurs me to tell you of Orpheus,
of Orpheus who transfixed the wild beasts with his singing
and made the inferno his servant by his entreaties:
immortal glory of Pindus and of Helicon.

Now, during my song, now happy, now lamenting,
let no bird move among these plants,
nor let there be heard any splashing wave upon these shores,
and let every breeze stop its movement.

ATTO II

Messaggiera:
Ahi, caso acerbo! Ahi, fat'empio e crudele!
Ahi, stelle ingiuriose! Ahi, ciel avaro!

Pastore:
Qual suon dolente il lieto dì perturba?

Messaggiera:
Lassa dunque debb'io
Mentre Ofeo con suo note il ciel consola,
Con le parole mie passargli il core.

Pastore:
Questa è Silvia gentile
Dolcissima compagna
Della bell'Euridice. O quanto è in vista
Dolorosa hor che sia? Deh sommi Dei,
Non torcete da noi benigno il guardo.

Messaggiera:
Pastor, lasciate il canto,
Ch'ogni nostra allegrezza in doglia è volta.

Orfeo:
D'onde vieni? Ove vai? Ninfa che porti?

Messaggiera:
A te ne vengo Orfeo
Messaggiera infelice
Di caso più infelice e più funesto.
La tua bella Euridice

Orfeo:
Ohimè, che odo?

Messaggiera:
La tua diletta sposa è morta.

Orfeo:
Ohimè.

ACT II

Messenger:
Ah, bitter news! Alas, harsh and cruel fate!
Ah, injurious stars! Ah, miserly heaven!

Shepherd:
What sorrowful sound disturbs our happiness?

Messenger:
Alas, it falls to me,
while Orfeo with his notes consoles heaven,
with my words to stab him in the heart.

Shepherd:
This is gentle Silvia,
sweetest companion
of the beautiful Eurydice. Oh, how sorrowful is her
expression. Now what is it? Oh, gods above,
do not turn from us your benign gaze.

Messenger:
Shepherd, leave off your singing.
All of our happiness is turned to sorrow.

Orpheus:
Where did you come from? Where are you going?
What do you bring, Nymph?

Messenger:
To you I come, Orpheus,
an unhappy messenger
of news utterly unhappy and utterly tragic.
Your beautiful Eurydice....

Orpheus:
Oh no, what am I hearing?

Messenger:
Your delightful bride is dead.

Orpheus:
Oh no!

Messaggiera:
In un fiorito prato
Con l'altre sue compagne
Giva cogliendo fiori
Per farne una ghirlanda a la sue chiome,
Quand'angue insidioso
Ch'era fra l'erbe ascoso,
Le punse un piè con velenoso dente.
Ed ecco immantinente
Scolorirsi il bel viso e nei suoi lumi
Sparir que lampi con'ella al sol fea scorno.
All'hor noi tutte sbigottite e meste
Le fummo intorno più richiamar tentando
Li spirti in lei smarriti
Con l'onda fresca e con possenti carmi,
Ma nulla valse ahi lassa
Ch'ella i languidi lumi al quanto aprendo
E te chiamando Orfeo.
Dopo un grave sospiro
Spirò fra queste braccia ed io rimasi
Piena il cor di pietade e di spavento.

Pastore:
Ahi caso acerbo! Ahi fat'empio e crudele!
Ahi stelle ingiuriose, ahi ciel avaro.

Pastore:
A l'amara novella
Rassembra l'infelice un muto sasso,
Che per troppo dolor non può dolersi.
Ahi ben havrebbe un core di tigre o d'orsa
Chi non sentisse del tuo mal pietate,
Privo d'ogni tuo ben misero amante.

Orfeo:
Tu se' morta, mia vita, ed io respiro?
Tu se' da me partita
Per mai più non tornare ed io rimango?
Nò, se i versi alcuna cosa ponno
N'andrò sicuro a più profondi abissi,
E intenerito il cor del Rè del'ombre,

Meco trarroti a riveder le stelle.
O se ciò negherammi empio destino
Rimarrò teco in compagnia di morte.
A Dio terra, a Dio cielo, e Sole a Dio.

Messenger:
In a flowering meadow,
with others of her companions,
she went about collecting flowers
to make a garland for her hair,
when a treacherous snake,
which was hidden in the grass,
bit her foot with its poisonous fangs.
And behold! Suddenly
her beautiful face lost its color,
and the light went out of her eyes, which made the
sun envious. Then all of us, shocked and grieving,
gathered around her, calling back
the spirit that had left her
with cool water and powerful incantations.
But nothing availed, alas!
And she, with languid eyes, as I could see,
called out to you, "Orpheus!"
After a deep sigh,
she expired in my arms, and I remained
with my heart full of pity and fear.

Shepherd:
Ah, bitter news! Ah, harsh and cruel fate! Ah, injurious stars! Ah, miserly heaven!

Shepherd:
At such bitter news
this unhappy man resembles a speechless stone,
who, for too much sorrow, cannot lament.
Ah, he would have the heart of a tiger or of a bear
who did not feel pity for his misfortune,
deprived of everything good, a miserable lover.

Orpheus:
You are dead, my life, and I breathe?
You are departed from me,
never more to return, and I remain?
No! For if verse can do anything,
I will go, secure, to the depths of the abyss,
and, making tender the heart of the King of the
Shadows,
with me you will return to again see the stars.
Or, if that be denied me by cruel destiny,
I will remain with you in the company of death.
Farewell earth; farewell sky, and Sun, farewell.

11 FRANCESCA CACCINI, *La liberazione di Ruggiero dall'isola d'Alcina* (1625), excerpt

from the printed score (Florence, 1625)

Melissa:
Ecco l'ora, ecco il punto
Da tra di servitù l'alto guerriero,
Ecco il giorno fatale omai, ch'è giunto
Sorgi, sorgi Ruggiero.

Ruggiero:
Qual'importuna voce
Disturba i miei riposi?

Melissa:
This is the hour, this is the moment
to end the servitude of the noble warrior,
this is the fateful day at last:
arise, arise, Ruggiero!

Ruggiero:
What rude voice
disturbs my repose?

Melissa:
Atlante a te se'n viene
Per saper qual follia
Ti sforza ad infamarti in queste arene.
De miei lunghi sudori
Questi frutti raccogli?
Tra militari ardori
Tutta avvampa la terra,
Va tutta Libia, e tutta Europa in guerra;
Ogn'animo più forte
Sprezza rischi di morte,
E tu mal consigliato,
Ami da sozza Maga esser'amato?
Impudico Ruggiero,
Ov'è l'invitta spada
Ov'è il lucido acciaro,
Che ti rendeo si chiaro?
Rimira di quai fregi,
Di quai profani carmi
Hai macchiate quell'armi?
Ruggiero il vincitore
Sacra ad Alcina il cor, l'armi ad amore
Togli folle, che sei
Alle braccia guerriere,
Et al collo viril monili, e vezzi,

Lascia l'iniqua Maga,
E muovi ad affrontar nemiche schiere
Se la bell'alm'ancor di gloria è vaga.

Ruggiero:
Lasso me che purtroppo
Conosco il mio fallire,
Ma no'l vorrei mirar senza morire,
Fierissimo dolore
Asprissimo tormento,
Che quinci intorno al core.
La vergogna accrescete e'l pentimento,
Fatemi guerra ogn'ora,
Agitatemi voi tanto ch'io mora.
Itene a terra parte
Vane pompe d'amore
Al braccio torni di nuovo il chiaro scudo,
E'l fortissimo usbergo il petto adorni.
Perdona, al fallo indegno
Ò mio custode, e Padre,
Più non ardo d'amore ardo di sdegno,
E bramo d'assalir guerriere squadre.

Melissa:
Atlante has come
that you might know what folly
compels you to dishonor yourself upon these shores.
Are these the fruits
of my long labors?
Amidst raging armies
abroad in the land,
all of Libya and all of Europe are at war,
every courageous soul
risks death,
while you, ill advised,
love this foul witch in order to be loved?
Shameless Ruggiero!
Where is the invincible sword?
Where is the shining archer?
What will make your mind clear?
Admiring those decorations
and those wicked spells,
have you sullied those weapons?
Ruggiero the conqueror,
you dedicate your heart and arms to Alcina for love.
Madman,
cast off from your warrior's arms
and from your manly neck these necklaces and charms.
Leave the evil sorceress
and confront the enemy troops
if you still have a soul desirous of glory.

Ruggiero:
Alas, I recognize
my error,
but I would not see it without dying
of the most painful sorrow
and the harshest torment
that weigh on my heart.
May my shame grow and my repentance.
Make me warlike at once:
spur me on to death.
Be gone,
vain glories of love.
My shining shield returns to my arm,
and that strong breastplate adorns my chest.
Pardon me for my unworthy error,
my protector and father,
I no longer burn to love, I burn with wrath,
and I long to attack the ranks of soldiers.

12 STEFANO LANDI, *Il S. Alessio* (1632), Act I, scenes 2–4

from the original printed score (Rome, 1634)

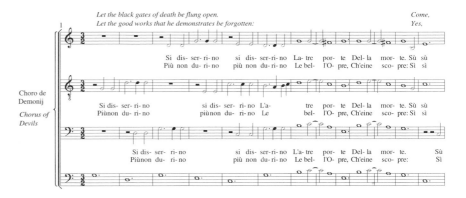

path. *Nor can he now withdraw himself from his companions,* *the sighs mixed with tears*

tie- ro: Nè de' con- giu- ni[?] suo- i Ho- mai ri- trar- re il pon- no I so- spir' con le la- gri- me in- ter- rot- ti,

with which, without food by day and sleep by night, he carries on. *O if only his tired body would rest*

Che sen- za ci- bo i gior- ni, e sen- za son- no Trag- ge in- tie- re le not- ti, O se tal'ho- ra ei po- sa il cor- po las- so,

with a hard rock for a pillow. *But if today I am nothing but what I have been,* *I will soften*

E sua mor- bi- da piu- ma un du- ro sas- so. Mà s'al- tro hog- gi non son da quel, ch'io so- glio, Ram- mol- li- rò quel

that heart of stone. *I, author of all deceit,* *spurred on by fierce disdain* *to the great undertaking,*

co- re D'a- da- man- ti- no sco- glio: Io d'o- gni fro- de au- to- re, Spin- to da fie- ro sde- gno al- l'al- ta im- pre- sa,

shall not spend my days and hours in indolence; *but, launching a sharp attack* *against his hard heart,*

Non trar- rò ne- ghit- to- so i gior- ni, e l'ho- re; Mà con- tra il du- ro pet- to Mo- ven- do a- spra con-

shall so hide my cunning under a false exterior *that I shall accomplish* *every part of my deception.*

te- sa, Sot- to men- ti- to a- spet- to Ce- le- rò co- sì l'ar- ti, Che d'o- gni fro- de a- dem- pi- rò le par- ti.

Choro de Demonij.
Continuandosi a cantare dientro all'Inferno,
i sopradetti Demoni fanno una Moresdca con
i tizzoni, che portano in mano.

Chorus of Devils
Continuing to sing
from behind the inferno,
the above mentioned devils dance a Moresca
with torches, which they carry in their hands

A terrible anger, *leads us up to*
If we are to seize *from a thousand souls*
The spirits are thundering, *the shores of*

Sde- gno hor- ri- bi- le sde- gno hor- ri- bi- le Al- la lu- ce
S'han- no a pren- de- re s'han- no a pren- de- re Di mil- le Al- me
L'om- bre tuo- ni- no l'om- bre tuo- ni- no; Fre- ma il li- to

the light. *Come, come,* *let the fearsome* *abyss* *take arms.*
their happy palms, *then* *let none spare himself in the attack.*
the Cocitus tremble. *Yes, yes,* *let fierce incantations resound.*

Ne con- du- ce. Sù sù sù sù sù sù sù ter- ri- bi- le L'a- bis- so s'ar- mi.
Lie- te pal- me: Già già già già già già d'of- fen- de- re Niun si ri- spiar- mi.
Di Co- ci- to. Sì sì sì sì sì sì ri- suo- ni- no Sol fie- rì car- mi.

To blows, to slaughter, to arms,

To blows, to slaughter, to arms, to arms!

SCENA SECONDA

Contemplando S. Alessio la vanità degli huomini, e la caducità della cose mondane, desidera di esser libero dalla carcere del Mondo, e perciò ricorre à Dio con l'oratione.

S. Alessio:
Sopra salde colonne erger che vale
Eccelse mura alle caduche spoglie,
Se poca terra al fine in sè n'accoglie?
O desir cieco, o vanità mortale.
O dal senso ingannati, e dal diletto
Lusingati desiri, io per mè trovo
Sotto alle patrie scale
Angusto sì, ma placido ricetto:
Quì soggiogando i sensi
A contemplar sovente il pensier muovo
Del cielo i regni immensi:
E spero ben, che questa ov'io mi copro,
Sarà scala al Fattor, s'io ben l'adopro.

Se l'hore volano,
E seco involano
Ciò, ch'altri hà quì;
Chi l'ali a mè darà;
Tanto ch'all'alto polo
Io prenda il volo,
e mi riposi là.

Nel mondo istabile,
altro durabile,
Ch'il duol non è;
Chi l'ali a mè darà.
Tanto ch'all'alto polo
Io prenda il volo,
e mi riposi là.

Quei rai, che splendono
Qui l'alme offendono,
Nè serban fè;
Chi l'ali a mè darà;
Tanto ch'all'alto polo
Io prenda il volo,
e mi riposi là.

SCENE II

St. Alexis, contemplating the vanity of men and the frailty of mortal things, wishes to be freed from the prison of this world, and therefore turns to God in prayer.

St. Alexis:
What is the use of erecting high walls
on massive columns for one's frail remains,
when a small patch of earth suffices to receive them?
Oh blind ambition, oh mortal vanity,
oh desires deluded by the senses and
charmed by pleasure! I for my part find
beneath my father's staircase
a lodging narrow, indeed, but tranquil:
here, subjugating my senses,
I often direct my thought to contemplating
the limitless realms of Heaven:
and I truly hope that this staircase beneath which I shelter
will, if I use it aright, be my staircase to the Creator.

Since the hours fly away
and bear off with them
what others possess down here,
who will give me wings,
so that to the highest pole
I may take flight
and there repose?

In this unstable world,
nothing is lasting
save grief;
who will give me wings,
so that to the highest pole
I may take flight
and there repose?

Those eyes that shine
down here offend the spirit
and do not keep faith;
who will give me wings,
so that to the highest pole
I may take flight
and there repose?

SCENA TERZA

S. Alessio, Maritio, Curtio, Paggi. Maritio e Curtio Paggi di Eufemiano, col vedere S. Alessio, stimato da loro un Forestiero mendico, e par carità alloggiato in quel Palazzo, non lasciano di schernirlo, ascoltati da S. Alessio con humiltà, e sofferenza.

Curtio & Martio:
Poca voglia di far bene,
Viver lieto, andar a spasso,
Fresc'e grasso
Mi mantiene.
La fatica M'è nemica;
E mentr'io vivo così,
È per me fest'ogni dì;
Diri Diri Diri

Vada il mondo come vuole,
lascio andar, nè mi molesto;
Tutto il resto
Son parole:
Pazzo è bene
Da catene,
chi fastidio mai si dà,
Per saper quel, che sarà.
Diri Diri Diri

Curtio:
Ma colà mesto e solitario io vedo
Quel Pellegrin mendico,
Ch'in questo Albergo il mio Signor mantiene;
E per quanto io mi credo,
Per nostro gusto il tiene:
Ch'ei quasi è mentecatto,
Honora chi l'offende,
Nè s'altri lo disprezza, a sdegno il prende.
Però qualunque volta in lui m'abbatto,
Hor con opre il dileggio, hor con parole,

E quasi folle al par di lui divento:
Perché ben dir si suole,
Ch'un matto ne fa cento.

SCENE III

St. Alexis, and the pages Martio and Curtio. Martio and Curtio, Eufemiano's pages, seeing St. Alexis and taking him for a foreign beggar given lodging in that palace out of charity, tease him remorselessly; St. Alexis listens to them with humility and patience.

Curtio & Martio:
Little wishing to do good,
but to lead a happy life and have fun,
keeps me
fresh and sleek.
Hard work is repugnant to me;
and so long as I can live like this,
every day is a holiday for me;
Diri Diri Diri

Let the world wag how it will,
I let it go, and don't care a jot;
all else
is just words:
and he's truly a madman
fit to lock up
who ever puts himself out
to think what the future will bring.
Diri Diri Diri

Curtio:
But over there I see, glum and all on his own,
that beggarly pilgrim
that my Master keeps in this house;
and so far as I can make out
he keeps him for our amusement:
for he is almost a half-wit,
reveres anyone who hurts him,
and won't lose his temper if someone insults him.
All the same, whenever I have a go at him,
sometimes I ridicule him with deeds, sometimes
with words
I end up becoming almost as crazy as he is;
which is why people say
that one madman makes a hundred others like him.

Martio:
Deh, qual mordace cura
T'offende, e per qual duolo
Porti la fronte oscura:
Onde quì te ne stai tacito, e solo.

S. Alessio:
Che altro far poss'io vile, e dimesso,
Io che son della terra inutil pondo,
Di mille colpe impresso,
Poi ch'altro non sò far, fuggo, e m'ascondo.

Curtio:
Non trattiam di fuggire,
che quella fuga sol gloria richiede,
Che si fa con la voce, e non col piede.

Martio:
Se vuoi mostrarti intrepido, e sicuro,
Odi che far dovresti.
Già si tocca tamburo:
Andiamo a pigliar soldo agili, e presti,
E con la piuma alteri,
Tosto fatti guerrieri
Passeggiarem con maestade il campo.

Martio:
Tell me, what biting cares
upset you, and what grief
darkens your brow,
so that you lurk about here silent and all alone?

St. Alexis:
What else can I do, worthless and base as I am,
I who am a useless clod of clay,
trampled by a thousand blows?
Since I can do nothing else, I run away and hide.

Curtio:
Lets not talk of running,
for the only runs that deserve honor
are made with the voice, and not with the feet.

Martio:
If you want to show how brave you are, but in safety,
I'll tell you what you ought to do.
When you hear them beating the drum,
Let's go, lithe and nimble, to enlist,
and then, proud of our plumed hats,
as soon as we're made soldiers,
we'll strut majestically about the parade ground.

S. Alessio:
A che cercar' in terra,
Di nuove guerre inciampo,
Sè la vita mortale anch'essa è guerra?

Curtio:
Discorsi cotant'alti
Io per me non intendo,
Mà molto ben comprendo,
Che da' nemici assalti
Tu sei stato chiarito,
Però fuggi l'invito.

Martio:
Costui per dirne il vero,
Alle parole, all'habito, al sembiante
Mi rassembra un soldato,
Che già deposto il minacciar primiero,
Ritorni svaligiato.

Curtio:
Se vuoi parer valente, altro bisogna;
Mà tù gloria non curi,
O gran vergogna.

Curtio & Martio:
O gran vergogna.

Martio:
Invero io tel confesso,
Quand'io ti sono appresso,
Sempre voglia mi viene
Darti la burla in fede mia, ma taccio.
Hor perchè tal pensiero
Mi si levi di mente,
Fa' che ti parta, vista la presente.

Curtio:
Tu che sei sì codardo,
con sollecito piè, con humil guardo
Di quì sgombra, e t'invola,
E senza più tardar, prendi altra via;

Martio & Curtio:
Vada Vosignoria.

St. Alexis:
Why seek on earth
the horrors of new wars,
since mortal life is itself warfare?

Curtio:
I for my part don't understand
such lofty speeches,
but I can see very clearly
that you know all about facing
hostile attacks,
but nevertheless refuse the challenge.

Martio:
To tell you the truth,
judging by his speech, his dress, and his face,
he looks like a soldier
who has lost all desire to fight
and fled home without a bean.

Curtio:
If you want to play the hero, that's not the way;
but you don't give a rap what people think of you:
it's shameful.

Curtio & Martio:
It's shameful.

Martio:
In truth I must confess
that when I'm near you
the desire comes over me
to make fun of you, I swear it; but I keep quiet.
Now in order to remove such a thought
from my mind,
respect my feelings and get away from here.

Curtio:
You who are such a coward,
clear off, remove yourself
with rapid step and meek aspect,
and without more ado, hop it!

Martio & Curtio:
Go, milord!

SCENA QUARTA
Demonio, Choro di demonii dentro alla Scena, Un'altro Choro, che balla. Sollecitato il Demonio dai Chori infernali, che promettendosi gran vittorie, fanno allegrezza con balli, si mette all'impresa di tentare, e sedurre la costanza del Santo. Si muta la Scena in un'Inferno; e nella lontananza si rappresentano le pene dei dannati. Si canta l'Aria, che segue, e da un Choro di Demonii è accompagnata con diverse mutanze.

Choro de Demonii:
Si disserrino
Latre porte
Dalla morte.
Sù, sù s'atterrino
D'Alessio i pregi.
Alle prede alle palme ai vanti ai fregi.

Più non durino
Le bell'opre,
ch'ei ne scopre:
Sì sì s'oscurino
Suoi fatti egregi.
Alle prede alle palme ai vanti ai fregi.

Demonio:
Dalla notte profonda,
Ove correndo il torbido Acheronte,
Unisce con terror la fiamma, e l'onda,
Pur' hoggi ergo la fronte,
A cenni mosso del tartareo Duce,
Mal mio grado, a mirar l'aversa luce;
Che se ben delle stelle,
Noi già dall'alto Regno
Fulminate cademmo alme rubelle
Restand'il vano ardir vinto, e deluso.
Non ancora però spento e lo sdegno,
Non anco in varco alle nostre armi e chiuso
Ben ch'a i segue di vita
Aspiri l'huomo è, la sua speme affissi
Non è non è smarrita
la forza degli abbissi,
Per ordir'à suo danno
Tradimento, rigor, forze, & inganno.

SCENE IV
The Devil, Chorus of devils off-stage. Another Chorus of dancers. Urged an by the infernal choirs, who promise themselves great victories and rejoice with dances, the Devil sets about the task of tempting the Saint and seducing him from his constancy. The scene changes to a Hell; and in the distance are shown the torments of the damned. The following aria is sung, and a chorus of Devils accompanies it with various scene changes.

Chorus of Devils:
Let the black gates
of death
be flung open.
Come, come let us destroy
Alexis's good name.
To plunder, to laurels, to honor, to glory!

Let the good works
that he demonstrates
be forgotten:
Yes, yes, let his noble acts
be extinguished.
To plunder, to laurels, to honor, to glory!

Devil:
From the profound darkness
where the troubled Acheron's flow
mingles fear with fire and water,
today I raise my head,
impelled by the commands of the ruler of Tartarus,
against my will, to behold the hostile daylight.
For although by our stars
we are, already by the highest realm,
condemned and stricken rebel souls,
vain ardor and defeat remain.
Our anger is not yet spent.
It has not yet passed from our embrace.
although man and his hopes
aspire to follow life,
the power of the underworld
is not eliminated,
to cause harm,
betrayal, cruelty, force, and deception.

Ed ecco hor più, d'ogn'altro, il suo pensiero
Rivolge Alessio ad onta pur di noi
Al celeste sentiero:
Nè de' congiuni suoi
Homai ritrare il ponno
I sospir' con le lagrime interroti,
Che senza cibo i giorni, e senza sonno
Tragge intiere le notti,
O se tal'hora ei possa il corpo lasso,
E sua morbida piuma un duro sasso.
Mà s'altro hoggi non son da quel, ch'io soglio,
Rammollirò quel core
D'adamantino scoglio:
Io d'ogni frode autore,
Spinto da fiero sdegno all'alta impresa,
Non trarò neghitoso i giorni, e l'hore;
Mà contra il duro petto
Movendo aspra contesa,
Sotto mentito aspetto
Celerò così l'arti,
che d'ogni frode adempirò le parti.

Continuandosi a cantare dietro all'Inferno, i sopradetti Demoni fanno una Moresca con i tizzoni, che portano in mano.

Choro de Demonii:
Sdegno horribile
Alla luce
Ne conduce.
Sù, sù, terrible
L'abisso s'armi.
Alle pugne, alle straggi, all'armi.

S'anno a prendere
Di mille alme
Liete palme:
Già già d'offendere
Niun si rispiarmi.
Alle pugne, alle straggi, all'armi.

L'ombre tuonino
Frema il lido
Di Cocito.
Sì sì risuonino
Sol fieri carmi.
Alle pugne, alle straggi, all'armi.

And behold, again, at every thought
Alexis turns, in spite of us,
to the heavenly path.
Nor can he now draw
from his companions
the sighs mixed with tears, with which
without food by day
and sleep by night, he carries on.
O, if only his tired body would rest
with a hard rock for a pillow.
But if today I am nothing but what I have been,
I will soften that
heart of stone.
I, author of all deceit,
spurred on by fierce disdain to the great undertaking,
shall not spend my days and hours in indolence;
but, launching a sharp attack
against his hard heart,
shall so hide my cunning
under a false exterior
that I shall accomplish every part of my deception.

Chorus of Devils continuing to sing from behind the inferno, the above mentioned devils dance a Moresca with torches, which they carry in their hands.

Chorus of Devils:
A terrible anger
leads us
up to the light.
Come, let the fearsome
abyss take arms.
To blows, to slaughter, to arms!

If we are to seize
from a thousand souls
their happy palms,
then let none spare himself
in the attack.
To blows, to slaughter, to arms!

The spirits are thundering,
the shores
of the Cocitus tremble.
Yes, yes, let
fierce incantations resound.
To blows, to slaughter, to arms!

13 CLAUDIO MONTEVERDI, *Hor ch'el ciel e la terra* (1638)

from his *Madrigali guerrieri, et amorosi . . . libro ottavo*

(Venice, 1638)

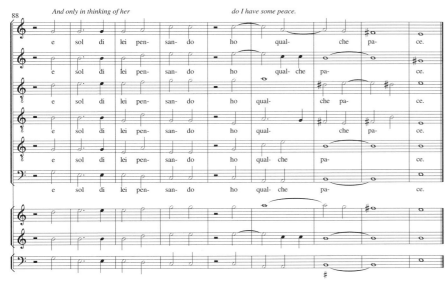

Seconda parte

Hor ch'el ciel e la terra e'l vento tace
E le fere e gli augelli il sono affrena,
Notte il carro stellato in giromena
E nel suo letto il mar senz'onda giace,
Veglio, penso, ardo, piango, e chi mi sface
Sempre m'innanzi, per la mia dolce pena:
Guerra è il mio stato d'ira e di duol piena
E sol di lei pensando ho qualche pace.
Così sol d'una chiara fonte viva
Move'l dolce e l'amaro, ond'io mi pasco;
Una man sola mi risana e punge.
E perchè'l mio martir non giunga a riva,
Mille volte al dì moro, e mille nasco:
Tanto de la salute mia son lunge.

Now that heaven and earth and wind are silent
and the beasts and the birds are deep in sleep,
Night circles in her starry chariot,
and the sea lies in its bed without waves,
I wake, I think, I burn, I weep, and she who undoes me
is always before me to my sweet pain.
War is my condition, full of anger and pain,
and only in thinking of her do I have any peace.
Thus, from a single, clear, living source
arise the bitter and sweet on which I feed.
A single hand cures me and stabs me,
and because my suffering does not reach its goal,
a thousand times a day I die and a thousand I am born:
so far off am I from my salvation.

14 GIOVANNI GIROLAMO KAPSBERGER, Toccata no. 5 (1604)

from his *Libro primo d'intavolatura di chitarone* (Venice, 1604)

15 GIROLAMO FRESCOBALDI, Toccata nona (1627)

from his *Il secondo libro di toccate, canzone, versi d'hinni,*
Magnificat, gagliarde, correnti, et altre partite d'intavolatura di
cimbalo et organo (Rome, 1627; 1/1637)

Non senza fatiga sì giunge al fine
Not without effort the end is reached

16 ALESSANDRO PICCININI, *Ciaconna in parteite variate* (1623)
from his *Intavolatura di liuto, et di chitarrone, libro primo*
(Bologna, 1623)

17 GIROLAMO FRESCOBALDI, *Partite sopra passacagli* (1627)

from his *Il secondo libro di toccate, canzone, versi d'hinni,*
Magnificat, gagliarde, correnti, et altre partite d'intavolatura di
cimbalo et organo (Rome, 1627; 1/1637)

18 GIOVANNI SALVATORE, *Versi sopra il Kyrie* (1641), with chanted verses added

from his *Ricercari a quattro voci, Canzoni francesi, toccate, et versi* (Naples, 1741)

19 ADRIANO BANCHIERI, *Fantasia prima* (1603)

from his *Fantasie overo canzoni alla francese per suonare nell'*
organo et altri stromenti musicali, a quattro voci (Venice, 1603)

20 GIROLAMO FRESCOBALDI, *Canzon quarti toni, dopo il post comune* (1635)

from his *Fiori musicali di diverse compositioni* (Venice, 1635)

21 GIOVANNI PAOLO CIMA, *Sonata, violino e violone* (1610)

from his *Concerti ecclesiastici* (Milano, 1610)

22 GIOVANNI BATTISTA FONTANA, Sonata 6 (before 1630)

from his *Sonate a 1. 2. 3. per il violino, o cornetto, fagotto,*
chitarone, violoncino o simile altro istromento (Venice, 1641)

23 BIAGIO MARINI, *Sonata sopra la monica* (1629)

from his *Sonate, symphonie, canzoni, pass'emezzi, baletti,*
corenti, gagliarde, & retornelli, a 1. 2. 3. 4. 5. & 6. voci,
per ogni sorte d'instrumenti, Op. 8 (Venice, 1626)

24 GIOVANNI BATTISTA BUONAMENTE, Sonata quarta (1626)

from his *Il quarto libro de varie sonate, sinfonie, gagliarde,*

corrente, e brandi . . . (Venice, 1626)

25 MARCO UCCELLINI, *Sonata prima a violino solo detta la vittoria trionfante* (1645)

from his *Sonate, correnti, et aire da farsi con diversi stromenti*

si da camera, come da chiesa, a uno, a due, et a tre, opera quarta

(Venice, 1645)

26 MARCO DA GAGLIANO, *Vinea mea electa* (ca. 1610)

from his *Responsoria maioris hebdomadae quatuor paribus*

vocibus decantanda Marci a Gagliano (Venice, 1630)

Vinea mea electa, ego te plantavi
Quomodo conversa es in amaritudinem,
ut me crucifigeres, et Barabbam dimitteres?
Sepivi te et lapides elegi ex te et edificavi turrim.

My chosen vine, I planted you.
How could you turn out bitter,
that you should crucify me and release Barabbas?
I spaded you and cleared you of stones and built a watchtower.

27 LODOVICO VIADANA, *Duo seraphim clamabant* (1602)

from his *Cento concerti ecclasiastici, a una, a due, a tre, & a quattro voci, con il basso continuo per sonar nell'organo, nova inventione commoda per ogni sorte de cantori, & per gli organisti . . . opera duodecima* [1602], *quarta impressione* (Venice, 1605)

Duo seraphim clamabant alter ad alterum:
Sanctus, sanctus, sanctus,
Dominus, Deus Sabaoth:
Plena est omnis terra gloria ejus.
Tres sunt qui testimonium dant in caelo:
Pater, Verbum, et Spiritus Sanctus,
et hi tres unum sunt.
Plena est omnis terra gloria ejus.

Two angels called out to one another,
Holy, holy, holy,
Lord, God of hosts:
all the earth is full of his glory.
There are three who give testimony in heaven:
Father, Word, and Holy Spirit,
and these three are one.
All the earth is full of his glory.

28 CATERINA ASSANDRA, *O salutaris hostia* (1609)

from her *Motetti a due & tre voci . . . opera seconda*

(Milan, 1609)

O salutaris hostia,
Quae caeli pandis ostium,
Bella premunt hostilia,
Da robur, fer auxilium.
Alleluia.

O, salutary host,
which opens wide the door of heaven,
wars and enemies press us;
give strength, offer aid,
Alleluia.

29 CLAUDIO MONTEVERDI, *Nigra sum* (1610)

from his *Sanctissimae Verigini missa senis vocibus ac vesperae pluribus decantandae* (Venice, 1610)

Nigra sum sed formosa, filiae Jerusalem.
Ideo dilexit me Rex et introduxit me in cubiculum suum
et dixit mihi, surge amica mea et veni.
Iam hiems transiit imber abiit
et recessit flores apparuerunt in terra nostra.
Tempus putationis advenit.

Black I am, but lovely, daughters of Jerusalem.
Therefore the king loved me and brought me into his
chamber, and said to me, "Arise, my love, and come.
Already the winter and rains are past;
and flowers have appeared in our land.
The time of pruning is coming."

30 GIACOMO CARISSIMI, *Historia di Jephte* (before 1650)

from F:Pn, MSVm1 1.477

[Part II]

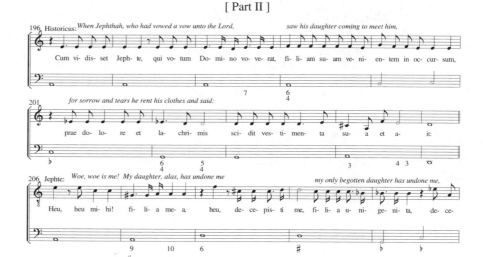

[PART I]

Historicus:
Cum vocasset in proelium filios Israel rex filiorum Ammon,
et verbis Jephte acquiescere noluisset,

factus est super Jephte Sprirtus Domini,
et progressus ad filios Ammon
votum vovit Domino dicens:

Jephte:
Si tradiderit dominus filios Ammon in manus meas

quicumque primus de domo mea occurrerit mihi,
offeram illum Domino in holocaustum.

Chorus:
Transivit ergo Jephte ad filios Ammon,
ut in spiritu forti et virtute Domini pugnaret contra eos.
Et clangebant tubae et personabant tympana,

et proelium commissum est adversus Ammon.
Fugite, cedite impii, perite gentes occumbite in gladio.
Dominus exercituum in proelium surrexit
et pugnat contra vos.
Fugite, cedite impii, corruite et in furore gladii dissipamini.

Chorus:
Cantemus onmes Domino, laudemus bellis principem,
qui dedit nobis gloriam et Israel victoriam.

[PART I]

Narrator:
When the king of the sons of Ammon called the sons of Israel
to battle, and would not agree to the words of Jephthah, the
spirit of the Lord came upon Jephthah,
and, having gone forth to the sons of Ammon,
he made a vow unto the Lord, saying:

Jephthah:
If the Lord will deliver into my hands the sons of Ammon,
whosoever comes first from my house to greet me,
him will I offer unto the Lord as a burnt offering.

Chorus:
Then Jephthah went over to the sons of Ammon,
so that, in a bold spirit and the strength of the Lord, he might
fight against them. And the trumpets blared, and the drums
beat, and the battle was begun against Ammon.
Flee, yield, impious ones; perish, heathens; fall on the sword;
the Lord of Hosts has risen up to battle and fights against you.
Flee, yield, impious ones. Sink down and scatter under the fury of our swords.

Chorus:
Let us all sing unto the Lord, let us praise the Prince of battle, who gave us glory and Israel the victory.

[PART II]

Historicus:
Cum vidisset Jephte, qui votum Domino voverat,
filiam suam venientem in occursum,
prae dolore et lachrimis scidit vestimenta sua et ait:

Jephte:
Heu mihi! Filia mea,
heu, decepisti me, filia unigenita,
heu filia mea decepta es.

Filia:
Cur ego te, pater decepi,
et cur ego filia tua unigenita decepta sum?

Jephte:
Aperuit os meum ad Dominum,
et quicumque primus de domo mea occurrerit mihi,
offeram illum Domino in holocaustum.
Heu mihi! Filia mea,
heu decepisti me, filia unigenita, decepisti me,
et tu pariter, heu filia mea, decepta es.

Filia:
Pater mi, si vovisti votum Domino
reversus victor ab hostibus,
ecce ego filia tua unigenita,
offero me in holocaustum victoriae tuae.
Hoc solum pater mi,
praesta filiae tuae unigenitae ante quam moriar.

Jephte:
Quid poterit animam tuam,
quid poterit te, moritura filia, consolari?

Filia:
Dimitte me, ut duobus mensibus circumeam montes,
ut cum sodalibus meis plangam virginitatem meam.

Jephte:
Vade filia, mea unigenita et plange virginitatem tuam.

[PART II]

Narrator:
When Jephthah, who had vowed a vow unto the Lord, saw his daughter coming to meet him, with sorrow and tears he rent his garments and said:

Jephthah:
Woe, woe is me! My daughter, alas, has undone me,
my only begotten-daughter, you have undone me,
and you, too, alas, my daughter, are also undone.

Daughter:
Why, father, have I undone you, and why am I, your only-begotten daughter, undone also?

Jephthah:
I opened my mouth unto the Lord, that whosoever
should come first from my house to greet me,
him Iwill I offer unto the Lord as a burnt offering.
Woe is me! my daughter, woe,
you have undone me, my only-begotten daughter;
and you likewise, woe, my daughter, are undone.

Daughter:
My father, my father, if you have vowed unto the Lord and have returned a victor from the enemy, here
I am, your only-begotten daughter,
I offer myself as a burnt offering for your victory.
Just this, my father, grant to me,
your only-begotten daughter, before I die.

Jephthah:
What can console your spirit, what can console you, my daughter, who are about to die?

Daughter:
Allow me for two months to go about the mountains with my companions bewailing my virginity.

Jephthah:
Go my daughter, go, my only-begotten daughter, and lament your virginity.

Chorus:
Abiit ergo in montes filia Jephte,
et plorabat cum sodalibus virginitatem suam, dicens:

Fillia:
Plorate, colles; dolete, montes,
et in afflictione cordis mei ululate!

Echo:
Ulutate!

Filia:
Ecce moriar virgo et non potero morte mea meis filliis
consolari. Ingemiscite silvae, fontes, et flumina; in interitu
virginis lachrimate, fontes et flumina, in interitu virginis lachrimate!

Echo:
Lachrimate!

Filia:
Heu me dolentem in laetitia populi, in victoria Israel et gloria
patris mei, ego sine filiis virgo, ego, filia unigenita moriar et
non vivam. Exhorrescite, rupes, obstupescite, colles, valles et
cavernae in sonitu horribili resonate!

Echo:
Resonate.

Filia:
Plorate filii Israel, plorate virginitatem mea et Jephte

filiam unigenitam in carmine doloris lamentamini.

Chorus:
Then the daughter of Jephthah went into the mountains, and bewailed her virginity with her companions, saying:

Daughter:
Weep, hills; grieve, mountains, and in the afflictions of my heart, moan!

Echo:
Moan!

Daughter:
Behold, I shall die a virgin, and may not in my death find
consolation in my children. Groan, forests, springs, and rivers,
at the death of a maiden springs and rivers, weep!

Echo:
Weep!

Daughter:
Woe, that I should sorrow in the joy of my people, in the
victory of Israel and the glory of my father. I, child-less, I, the
only-begotten daughter, shall die and not live! Shudder, rocks,
be astonished, hills and valleys, and caves, resound in horror!

Echo:
Resound!

Daughter:
Weep, weep, children of Israel, weep for my virginity, and
lament the only-begotten daughter of Jephthah in a song of sorrow.

Chorus:
Plorate filii Israel,
Plorate omnes virgines, et filiam Jephte unigenitam

in carmine doloris lamentamini.

Chorus:
Weep, children of Israel,
weep, all virgins, and lament the only-begotten daughter of Jephthah
in a song of sorrow.

31 GIOVANNI GABRIELI, *In ecclesiis* (ca. 1605)
from his *Symphoniae sacre . . . liber secundus . . . editio nova*
(Venice, 1615)

In ecclesiis benedicite Domino.
Alleluia.
In omni loco dominationis benedic anima mea
Dominum.
Alleluia.
In Deo salutari meo et gloria mea.
Deus auxilium meum et spes mea in Deo est.
Alleluia.
Deus meus, te invocamus, te adoramus.
Libera nos, salva nos, vivifica nos.
Alleluia.
Deus adjutor noster in aeternam.
Alleluia.

In all churches, praise the Lord.
Alleluia.
In every place of power bless, my soul, the Lord.

Alleluia.
In God is my salvation and my glory.
God is my help, and my hope is in God.
Alleluia.
My god, we call upon you, we worship you.
Free us. Save us. Give us life.
Alleluia.
God is our judge into eternity.
Alleluia.

32 LAMBERT DE BEAULIEU, *Balet comique de la Royne* (1581), Dialogue between Glauque and Tethys from Intermedio I

from the printed score, (Paris, 1582), which omits the accompaniment of this and several other solo-voice numbers; barlines have been added and note values have been halved.

La reprise du dialogue *The refrain of the dialogue*

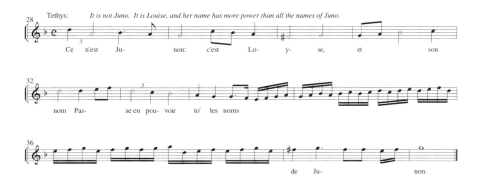

It is not Juno. It is Louise, and her name has more power than all the names of Juno.

Ce n'est Ju- non: c'est Lo- y- se, et son nom Pas- se en pou- voir to' les noms de Ju- non.

Glauque:
Mais que me sert Tethys ceste escaille nouvelle,
Que je suis d'un pescheur en dieu marin formé?

Je voudrois n'estre Dieu et de Scylle estre aymé,
Pour ne bruler en vain d'une flamme crudelle.

Moy qui fus immortel, ayant mangé d'une herbe,
Des herbes i'esprouvay la force & le pouvoir;
Pensant quelque secours en amour recevoir,
Le m'en allay vers Circe envieuse & superbe:

Les forests couvriront plustost le mer d'ombrage
Qu'on me puisse du coeur ceste Scylle arracher.
Sus, Dauphin, car le veux aller Scylle chercher,
Pitoyable Dauphin coupe les flots & nage.

Circe, jalouse Circe, indigne qui te nammes
Fille du Dieu qui tient le grand flambeau des cieux,

Oses-tu maintenant ensorceler les Dieux,
Toy qui soulois devant ne charmer que les hommes?

Les Dieux ont des humains la priere agreable,
Qui chargent leurs autels d'offrandes & flambeaux.

Escoute moy, Tethys, divinié des eaux,
Et à moy Dieu marin sois helas secourable!

Tethys:
L'arc d'Amour est victorieux
Contre les hommes et les Dieux,
Et de ses traits la blessure à chacun
Qui la reçoit apporte un mal commun.

Glaucus:
What good, Thethys, is this new shell,
Now that I have been changed from a fisherman into a sea god?

I would like not to be a god, and to be loved by Scylla,
in order not to be consumed by a cruel fire.

I became immortal because I ate an herb.
I felt the strength and power of the herb.
Hoping to receive some aid against Love,
I went to envious and proud Circe.

The forests will cover the whole sea with shade,
sooner than Scylla will be torn from my heart.
Come, Dolphin, I wish to search for Scylla.
Compassionate Dolphin, cut the waves and swim.

Circe, jealous Circe, unworthy to be
daughter of the god who controls the great flame in the sky,
do you dare to enchant gods,
you who were accustomed to enchant only men?

The gods have the prayers of humans,
who pile their altars high with offerings and with candles.
Harken to me, Tethys, divinity of water,
and help me, a sea-god.

Thethys:
The bow of Love is victorious
over men and gods.
And the marks of its wounds
bring the same suffering to all who are smitten.

Le coeur des flammes surmonté,
N'est point jamais tant irrité,
Qu'il est alors qu'en vain il s'est offert,
Et qu'un refus, honteux, il a souffert.

Circe a ta Scylle par venin
Changée en un rocher marin
Jusqu'au nombril, & ses pied abysmez
Dessous les flots sont en chiens transformez.

Les corps en esprit animez
Sont par Circe en monstres formez
Si tost qu'ils ont gousté de sa poison,
Tandis qu'ils sont privez de la raison.

Je n'ay dessus le eaux pouvoir
Ainsi que la soulois avoir;
Car ceste nymphe a recu de ma main
Dessus le eaux lo pouvoir souverain.

[Chorus:]
Et de ses traits la blessure à chacun
Qui la reçoit apporte un mal commun.

Glauque:
Et qui est ceste Nymphe?
Est ce une Nereide?

Tethys:
Non car la mer l'a point telle Nymphe conceu.

Glauque:
Je scay bien c'est Venus.

Tethys:
Tu es encor déçue. Elle a chasé Venus
dans les jardins de Gnide.

Glauque:
C'est donc Junon.

Tethus:
Tu te déçois.

Glauque:
Est'ce la Junon des François?

Tethys:
Ce n'est Junon: c'est Loyse,
et son nom Passe en pouvoir
to' les noms de Junon.

The inflamed heart
is never so much irritated
as when it has offered vainly
and has suffered a shameful rejection.

Circe has by her venom
changed your Scylla into a rock
as far as her waist, and her feet buried
in the water have been transformed into dogs.

The bodies of the living
are transformed by Circe into monsters
when they have tasted her poison,
they are deprived of their reason.

I have no power above the water,
as I used to have,
for this nymph has received from my own hand
the sovereign power above the waves.

[Chorus:]
And the marks of its wounds
bring the same suffering to all who are smitten.

Glaucus:
And who is the nymph?
Is she a Nereid?

Thethys:
No, for the sea has given birth to no nymph.

Glaucus:
I know. It is Venus.

Thethys:
You are still wrong. She has given Venus back
to the gardens of Cnidos.

Glaucus:
Then it is Juno.

Thethys:
You are wrong.

Glaucus:
Is it the French Juno?

Thethys:
It is not Juno. It is Louise,
and her name has more power than
all the names of Juno.

33 PIERRE FRANCISQUE CAROUBEL, Passameze and Gaillarde (before 1611)

from Michael Praetorius, ed., *Terpsichore, musarum*

aoniarum quinta (Wolfenbüttel, 1612)

Passameze

Gaillarde

34 MICHEL MAZUEL, Dances from the *Ballet du roy des festes de Baccus* (1651)

from D:Kl, Mus. vol. 61, I, D3

Courante

Sarabande

Bourée

Bourée

35 ANON., *Ma bella si ton ame* (1603)

from *Thesaurus harmonicus divini Laurencini Romani*
(Cologne, 1603)

Du soleil la lumiere
Sur le soir se desteint,
Puis à l'aube premiere
Elle reprend son teint.
Mais nostre jour,
Quant une foys il tombe,
Demeure soub la tombe,
Y faisant long séjour.

The light of the sun
extinguished in the evening
at first dawn
recovers its hue;
but our day
once fallen,
remains beneath the tomb,
taking there its long rest.

Et puis ces ombres saintes,
Hostesses da là-bas,
Ne démentent qu'en feintes
Leurs amoureux esbatz.
Entre elle plus
Amour n'a de puissance,
Et plus n'ont jouissance
Des plaisirs de Vénus.

And those hallowed shades,
visitors from below,
can only pretend to revel
in love's delights;
amongst them
love is impotent,
and they no longer take joy
in the pleasures of Venus.

Mais laschement couchées
Soub ces myrtes pressés,
Elles pleurent faschées
Leurs ages mal passés,
Se lamentant
Que n'ayant plus de vie,
Encore ceste envie
Les aille tourmentant.

But limply lying
beneath these crowded myrtles
they weep mournfully
over their wasted days,
lamenting that,
though they are without life,
envy still
torments them.

Ma belle si ton ame
Se sent or' allumer
De ceste douce flame
Qui nous force d'aymer,
Allons contans,
Allons sur la verdure,
Allons tandis que dure
Nostre jeune printemps.

My beauty, if your soul
already feels on fire
with that sweet flame
that forces us to love,
let us go then,
let us go upon the grass,
let us go while
our young springtime lasts.

Avant que la journée
De nostre age qui fuit
Se sente environée
Des ombres de la nuit,
Prenons loysir
De vivre nostre vie,
Et sans craindre l'envie
Baisons nous à plaisir.

Before the day
of our fleeting youth
finds itself engulfed
by the shades of night,
let us take time
to live our life,
and fearless of envy
let us kiss as we will.

Aymons donc à nostre aise,
Baisons, baisons nous fort,
Puisque plus l'on ne baise
Depuis que l'on est mort.
Voyons nous pas
Comme jà la jeunesse
Des plaisirs larronnesse
Fuit de nous à grand pas?

So let us love at our ease,
let us kiss passionately,
for we can kiss no more
after we are dead;
let us not see
how, already, youth,
with its purloined pleasures,
flees from us in haste.

Ça, finette affinée,
Ça, rompons le destin,
Qui clot nostre journée
Souvent des le matin.
Allons contans,
Allons sur la verdure,
Allons, tandis que dure
Nostre jeune printemps.

Artfully, then, let us
break with that destiny
that often ends our day
before it has begun;
let us go forth,
let us go upon the meadows,
let us go while
our young springtime lasts.

36 PIERRE GUÉDRON, *Quel excès de douleur* (1620)

from *Airs de cour mis en tablature de luth par Anthoyne Boesset . . . Neuviesme livre* (Paris, 1620)

Quel excès de douleur en cet éloignement,
Puisqu'il faut joindre encore à mon cruel tourment
Les peines du silence.
A quel soulagement doit un mal aspirer,
Où mesmes l'on deffend d'en pouvoir déclarer
L'extresme violence.

What an excess of sorrow in this separation!
because to my cruel torment are joined
the pains of silence.
To what solace can suffering aspire,
in which one cannot even declare
the extreme violence of it?

[Three strophes omitted]

Quoy! Vivray-je privé de cet allégement,
Ainsi que les damnés, sans voir du changement
En ma peine infinie?
Lucinde a des attraits qui charment ma raison
Et sçavent me contraindre en si belle prison
D'aymer sa tirannie.

What? Will I live deprived of this relief,
like the damned, with no change in sight
for my eternal suffering?
Lucinda has qualities that charm my mind
and know how to keep me in such a lovely prison,
and love her tyranny.

Elle voit sans pitié le cours de mes langueurs,
Rendant jusqu'aux enfer ses cruelle rigueurs
A mon ame fatalles,
Car je meurs esloignant cet objet désiré,
Et qui meurt hors de grace, est-il pas asseuré
Des peines infernalles?

She sees without pity the course of my yearnings,
delivering as far as Hell her cruel darts,
fatal to my soul.
So I die far from the object of my desire.
And whoever dies out of grace, is he not
assured of the agonies of Hell?

37 ANTOINE FRANCISQUE, Prelude and Courante (1600)

from his *Le trésor d'Orrphée* (Paris, 1600)

38 RENÉ MESANGEAU, Allemande from Lute (ca. 1630)

from *Tablature de luth de differens autheurs, sur les accords*
nouveaux (Paris, 1638)

39 ENNEMOND GAULTIER, *Tombeau de Mezangeau* (ca. 1638)

from F:Pn, Rés. 474

40 DENIS GAULTIER, *Mode Ionien* [suite for lute] (1648)

from D:Bk, Kupferstichkabinett, Mss. 78C12,

La rhètorique des dieux

[Sarabande]

La gaillard, The Saucy Lass

41 RENÉ MESANGEAU, Sarabande for Keyboard (ca. 1630)

from F:Pn, Rés. 89ter

42 JACQUES CHAMPION DE CHAMBONNIÈRES, Dances for Keyboard (ca. 1648)

from his *Les pièces de clavessin . . . livre second* (Paris, 1670)

43 EUSTACHE DU CAURROY, *Unziesme Fantasie* (1610)

from his *Fantasies, à III, IIII, V et VI parties* (Paris, 1610)

44 ÉTIENNE MOULINIÉ, Fantasie [for viols] (1639)

from his *Cinquiesme livre d'airs de cour quatre et cinq parties*

(Paris, 1639)

45 JEHAN TITELOUZE, *Magnificat Primi Toni* (1626)

from his *Le Magnificat ou Cantique de la Vierge pour toucher*
sur *l'orgue suivant les huit tons de l'Église* (Paris, 1626)

Quia Respexit

Et misericordia ejus

Deposuit potentes

Suscepit Israel

Gloria Patri et Filio

46 CHARLES RACQUET, Fantasie (ca. 1636)

from Marin Mersenne's personal copy of his *Harmonie universelle* (Paris, 1636)

47 EUSTACHE DU CAURROY, *Victimae paschali laudes* (1609)

from his *Preces ecclesiasticae ad numeros musices*

redactae . . . liber primus [secundus] (Paris, 1609)

"The tomb of Christ, who is living, the glory of Jesus's resurrection,

bright angels attesting, the shroud and vestment remaining.

Christ is risen, our hope.

He precedes us to Galilee.

Trust only in the truth of Mary

Victimae paschali laudes immolent Christiani.
Agnus redemit oves:
Christus innocens Patri reconciliavit peccatores.
Mors et vita duello conflixere mirando:

Dux vitae mortuus, regnat vivus.
Dic nobis, Maria, quid vidisti in via?
Sepulchrum Christi viventis
Et gloriam vidi resurgentis.
Angelicos testes, sudarium et vestes.

Surrexit Christus spes nostra;
praecedet suos in Galileam.
Credendum est magis soli Mariae veraci,
Quam Judaeorum turbae fallaci.
Scimus Christum surrexisse a mortuis vere.
Tu nobis, victor Rex, miserere. Alleluya.

To the paschal victim offer your praises, Christians.
A lamb redeems us.
Christ without sin reconciles sinners to the Father.
Death and life have contended in that stupendous
combat.
The Prince of life, who died, reigns immortal.
Tell us, Mary, what did you see along the way?
"The tomb of Christ, who is living,
the glory of Jesus's resurrection,
bright angels attesting, the shroud and vestment
remaining.
Christ is risen, our hope.
He precedes us to Galilee.
Trust more in truthful Mary
rather than the lying crowd of Jews.
We know that Christ is truly risen from the dead.
You, victorious King, have mercy on us. Alleluya!

48 GUILLAUME BOUZIGNAC, *Ecce homo* (ca. 1640)

from F;TOm, Ms. 168

Ecce homo.	Here is the man.
Crucifige eum.	Crucify him!
Regem vestrum crucifigam?	Shall I crucify your king?
Tolle, tolle, crucifige eum.	Away with him, away with him, crucify him!
Quid enim mali fecit?	What evil has he done?
Crucifige eum.	Crucify him!
Ecce Rex vester!	Here is your king!
Non habemus Regem nisi Caesarem!	We have no king but Caesar.
Dimittam illum in Pascha?	Shall I release him for Passover?
Non hunc, sed Barabbam!	Not him, but Barabbas!
Quid faciem de Jesu?	Then what shall I do with Jesus?
Tolle, tolle, crucifige eum.	Away with him, away with him, crucify him!

49 GREGOR AICHINGER, *Tres sunt qui testimonium dant* (1607)

from his *Cantiones ecclesiasticae* (Dillingen, 1607)

Tres sunt qui testimonium dant in caelo:
Pater, Verbum, et Spiritus Sanctus:
et hi tres unum sunt.
Sanctus, sanctus, sanctus.
Dominus Deus Sabaoth.
Plena est omnis terra gloria ejus.

There are three who bear witness in heaven:
Father, Word, and Holy Spirit:
and these three are one.
Holy, holy, holy.
Lord God of hosts,
All the earth is full of His glory.

50a NIKOLAS HERMAN, "Erschienen ist der herrliche Tag," chorale (1560)

Erschienen ist der herrliche Tag
Dran sich niemand gnug freuen mag.
Christ unser Herr heut triumphiert,
All sein Feind er gefangen führt.
Halleluja!

It has arrived, the glorious day,
for which no one can rejoice enough.
Christ our Lord today triumphs.
His enemy he has defeated.
Halleluja!

50b JOHANN HERMANN SCHEIN, *Eschienen ist der herrliche Tag* (1626)

from his *Opella nova, Ander Theil Geistlicher Concerten* (Leipzig, 1626)

Erschienen ist der herrliche Tag
Dran sich niemand gnug freuen mag.
Christ unser Herr heut triumphiert,
All sein Feind er gefangen führt.
Halleluja!

It has arrived, the glorious day,
for which no one can rejoice enough.
Christ our Lord today triumphs.
All His enemy are defeated.
Halleluja!

51 HEINRICH SCHÜTZ, *O quam tu pulchra,* SWV 165 (1629)

from his *Symphoniae sacrae . . . opus ecclasiasticum secundum*

(Venice, 1629)

119

Secunda Pars

Sinfonia

O quam tu pulchra es,
amica mea, columba mea, formosa mea, immaculata
mea! O quam tu pulchra es!
Oculi tui columbarum.
O quam tu pulchra es!
Capilli tui sicut greges caprarum.
O quam tu pulchra es!
Dentes tui sicut greges tonsarum.
O quam tu pulchra es!
Sicut vitta coccinea labia tua.
O quam tu pulchra es!
Sicut turris David collum tuum.
O quam tu pulchra es!
Duo ubera tua sicut duo hinnuli capreae gemelli.
O quam tu pulchra es!

Veni de Libano, veni,
amica mea, columba mea, formosa mea,
o quam tu pulchra es!
Veni, coronaberis.
Surge, propera,
amica mea, soror mea, sponsa mea, immaculata mea,
et veni.
O quam tu pulchra es!

O how beautiful you are,
my friend, my dove, my lovely, my immaculate one!
O how beautiful you are!
Your eyes are like the eyes of doves.
O how beautiful you are!
Your hair is like a flock of sheep.
O how beautiful you are!
Your teeth are like new-shorn ewes.
O how beautiful you are!
Like scarlet ribbons are your lips.
O how beautiful you are!
Like the tower of David your neck.
O how beautiful you are!
Your two breasts are like two fawns, twins of a gazelle.
O how beautiful you are!

Come from Lebanon, come,
my beloved, my dove, my lovely one,
O how beautiful you are!
Come, garland your brow.
Arise, make haste,
my beloved, my sister, my bride, my immaculate one,
and come.
O how beautiful you are!

52 HEINRICH SCHÜTZ, *Was hast du verwirket*, SWV 307 (1639)

from his *Anderer Theil kleiner geistlichen Concerten*

(Dresden, 1639)

Was hast du verwirket,
o, du allerholdseligster Knab, Jesu Christe,
daß du also verurteilt warest?
Was hast du begangen,
o du allerfreundlichster Jüngling,
daß man so übel und kläglich mit dir gehandelt?
Was ist doch dein Verbrechen und Mißhandlung?
Was ist deine Schuld,
was ist die Ursach deines Todes?
Was ist doch die Verwirkung deiner Verdammnis?
O, ich ben die Ursach und Plage deines Leidens,
ich bin die Verschuldung deines Hinrichstens,
ich bin das Verdienst deines Todes,
das todwürdige Laster, so an dir gerochen worden.
Ich bin die Öffnung der Wunden deines Leidens,
die Angst deiner Peinigung.
Ach, wohin, du Sohn Gottes,
hat sich deine Demut geniedriget?

What have you done,
oh, you sweetest child, Jesus Christ,
that you were condemned?
What have you committed,
oh, you gentlest youth,
than you are so cruelly and wretchedly treated?
What, then, is your crime and your transgression?
What is your guilt?
What is the reason for your death?
What, then, is the cause of your condemnation?
O, I am the cause and the torment of your suffering.
I bear the guilt for your execution.
I am the agent of your death,
the monstrous depravity that was thought to be in you.
I am the opening of the wounds of your suffering,
the anguish of your torture.
Ah, why, you Son of God,
did your humility demean itself?

53 HEINRICH SCHÜTZ, *Saul, Saul, was verfolgst du mich,* SWV 415 (1650)

from his *Symphoniarum sacrarum tertia pars* (Dresden, 1650)

Saul, Saul, was verfolgst du mich?
Es wird der schwer werden, wider den Stachel zu lökken.

Saul, Saul, why do you persecute me?
It will be hard to kick off the traces.

54 JAN PIETERSZOON SWEELINCK, *Ricercar del nono duono* (ca. 1610)

from I:Pu, MS 1982

55a Chorale "Ich ruf zu dir, herr Jesu Christ"

Ich ruf zu Dir, Herr Jesu Christ,
ich bitt, erhör mein Klagen,
verleih mir Gnad zu dieser Frist,
laß mich doch nicht verzagen.
Den rechten Glauben, Herr, ich mein,
den wollest Du mir geben,
Dir zu leben, mein'm
Nächsten nutz zu sein,
Dein Wort zu halten eben.

I call to Thee, Lord Jesus Christ,
I pray Thee hear my entreaty.
Grant me Grace in this life;
let me not despair.
For the right belief, Lord, I pray
that Thou grant me
to live in Thee,
to be of use in the next life,
to keep Thy word rightly.

55b SAMUEL SCHEIDT, *Fantasia à 4 Voc. super: ich ruffe zu dir, Herr Jesu Christ,*
SSWV 114 (1624) from his *Tabulatura nova*
continens variationes aliquot psalmorum, fantasiarum,

cantilenarum, passamezzo et canones (Hamburg, 1624)

56 JOHANN FROBERGER, Canzon (1649)

from A:Wn, MS 18706, "Libro secondo di toccate,
fantasie, canzone, allemande, courante, sarabande,
gigue et altre partite"

57 JOHANN FROBERGER, Allemand, Courant, & Saraband (1649)

from A:Wn, MS 18706, "Libro secondo di toccate,
fantasie, canzone, allemande, courante, sarabande, gigue
et altre partite"

Allemand

Courant

Saraband

58 PAUL PEUERL, Dances (1611)

from his *Newe Padouan, Intrada, Däntz, und Galliarda*

(Nürnberg, 1611)

XII. Galliarda

59 HEINRICH ALBERT, *O der rauhen Grausamkeit!* (1640)

from his *Ander Theil der Airen* (Königsberg, 1640)

Veneris miseras resonare querelas. Quam miserum est!
He complains loudly of his amorous woes. How miserable he is!

O der rauhen Grausamkeit?
Die nur seufzen jederzeit
Mit viel seufzen häuft.
O des Lebens ohne Leben
Das zum Tode läuft.
Das in zittern stets muß schweben
Trübsal, Kummer, Herzensglut
Solche Liebe geben tut.

Ist es denn der Sternen Kraft
Daß wir werden hingerafft
In die Dienstbarkeit?
Haben uns denn böse Stunden
Flammen zu bereit?
Flammen da nur wird gefunden.
Trübsal, Kummer, Herzensglut
Solche Liebe geben tut.

Wunderseltsam geht es zu:
Mann die Liebe schafft Unruh;
Wird's doch Ruh genandt?
Bey der Lieb' ist süsser Schmerzen
Kluger Unverstandt
Hark verknüpfft mit freyem Herzen.
Trübsal, Kummer, Herzensglut
Solche Liebe geben tut.

Oh, the harsh cruelty!
that only sighs constantly
with many sighs.
Oh, life without life
that to death hastens,
that in trembling it must hover.
Sorrow, care, heartache,
these love causes.

Is it, then, by the power of the stars
that we will be snatched away
into servitude?
Have evil hours, then,
prepared the flames for us?
Flames that now will be found.
Sorrow, care, heartache,
these love causes.

So strangely does it happen:
love makes one restless.
Will it, then, be called rest?
When in love, sweet sorrow is
clever madness
mixed with a free heart.
Sorrow, care, heartache,
these love causes.

60 JOHN JENKINS, Fantasia in Four Parts (ca. 1640)

from GB:Ob, MS C.99

61 JOHN COPRARIO, Fantasia–Suite no. 1 (ca. 1622)

from GB:Lbl, R. M. MS 24.K3 and GB: Ob, Music
MSS 732–34

62 JOHN DOWLAND, *The Frog Galliard* (ca. 1610)

from GB:Cu, Dd.2.11.(b)

63 JOHN LAWRENCE, *Coranto for Lute* (ca. 1625)
from "The Board Lute Book"

64 ORLANDO GIBBONS, *See, See, the Word Is Incarnate* (ca. 1620)

from GB:Lbl, Add. MSS 29372–77; and GB:Cch, 56–60

153

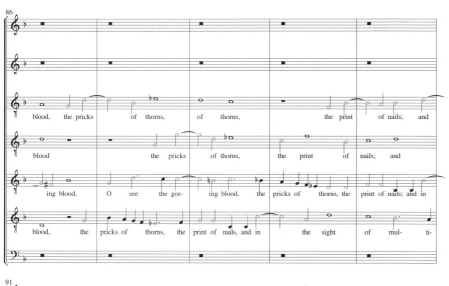

See, see, the word is incarnate;
God is made man in the womb of a virgin.
Shepherds rejoice, wise men adore, and angels sing:
Glory be to God on high: peace on earth, good will
towards men.
The Law is cancelled,
Jews and Gentiles all converted by the preaching of
glad tidings of salvation.
The blind have sight and cripples have their motion;
diseases cured, the dead are raised, and miracles are
wrought.
Let us welcome such a guest with Hosanna.
The paschal Lamb is offered,
Christ Jesus made a sacrifice for sin.
The earth quakes, the sun is darkened, the pow'rs of
hell are shaken;
and lo, He is risen up in victory.
Sing Alleluia.
O see the fresh wounds, the goring blood,
the pricks of thorns, the print of nails, and in the
sight of multitudes
a glorious ascension.
Where now He sits on God's right hand,
where all the choir of heav'n all jointly sing:
Glory be to the Lamb that sitteth on the throne.
Let us continue our wonted note with Hosanna:
Blessed be he that cometh in the name of the Lord;
with Alleluia we triumph in victory:
the serpent's head bruised, Christ's kingdom exalted,
and heav'n laid open to sinners. Amen.

65 JOHN DOWLAND, *Far from Triumphing Court* (1610)

from his *A Musicall Banquet, furnished with varietie of*

delicious ayres . . . (London, 1610)

Farre from triumphing Court and wonted glory,
He dwelt in shady unfrequented places,
Time's prisoner now, he made his pastime story,
Gladly forgets Court's erst afforded graces,
That Goddesse whom he served to heavn'n is gone,
And hee one earth, in darkness left to moane.

But loe a glorious light from his darke rest
Shone from the place where erst this Goddesse dwelt
A light whose beames the world with fruit hath blest
Blest was the Knight while hee that light beheld:
Since then a starre fixed on his head hath shinde,
And a Saint's Image in his hart is shrinde.

Ravisht with joy so grac't by such a Saint,
he quite forgat his Cell and selfe denaid,
He thought it shame in thankfulnesse to faint,
Debts due to Princes must be duely paid:
Nothing so hatefull to a noble minde,
As finding kindness for to prove unkinde.

But ah poore Knight though thus in dreame he ranged,
Hoping to serve this Saint in sort most meete,
Tyme with his golden locks to silver changed
Hath with age-fetters bound him hands and feete,
Aye me, hee cryes, Goddesse my limbs grow faint,
Though I time's prisoner be, be you my Saint.

66 FRANCESCO CAVALLI, *Giasone* (1649), excerpts

from I:Vmn, Ms. It IV–363

66a Act I, last scene

Medea:
Dell'antro magico
stridenti cardini,
il varco apritemi,
e fra le tenebre
del negro ospizio
lasciate mè.
Sù l'ara orribile
del lago stigio
i fochi splendino,
e in sù ne mandino
fumi che turbino
la luce al sol.

Da l'abbruciate glebe,
gran monarca dell'ombre intento ascoltami,
e se i dardi d'Amor già mai ti punsero,
adempi, ò Rè dei sotterranei popoli,
l'amoroso desio ch'e1 cor mi stimola,
e tutto Averno alla bell'opra uniscasi!
I mostri formidabili,
del bel vello di Friso
sentinelle feroci infaticabili,
per potenza d'Abisso
si rendono à Giasone oggi domabili.
Dall'arsa Dite
quante portate
(serpi alla fronte)
furie venite,
e di Pluto gl'imperi à mè svelate.
Già questa verga scuoto,
già percuoto
il suol col piè.

Horridi demoni,
spiriti d'Erebo,
volate à me!

Medea:
To the magic cave,
screeching hinges,
open the passage for me,
and amidst the darkness
of the black enclosure
let me pass.
On the horrible altar
by the waters of the
Styx let the flames
rise up and send forth
clouds of smoke to obscure
the light of the sun.

From your fiery glebes,
great monarch of the shades, hearken to me!
And if Love's darts have ever struck you,
fulfil, oh King of the Underworld,
the amorous desire that quickens my heart,
and let all Hades join in the fair deed.
Let the horrendous monsters,
the fierce, untiring sentinels
of Phrixos' lovely fleece
through the powers of the abyss
be subdued by Jason today.
From fiery Dis
you, who bear
serpents on your brows,
you Furies, come,
and reveal Pluto's kingdom to me!
Now I sway this wand
and already the earth
quakes beneath our feet!

Fearful demons,
spirits of Erebus,
fly to me!

Così indarno vi chiamo?
Quai strepiti,
quai sibili
non lascian penetrar nel cieco baratro
le mie voci terribili?
Dalla sabbia
di Cocito
tutta rabbia
quà v'invito.
Al mio soglio
quà vi voglio;
à che si tarda più?
Numi tartarei, sù!

Coro di spiriti:
Le mura si squarcino,
le pietre si spezzino,
le moli si franghino,
vacillino, cadano,
e tosto si penetri
ove Medea si stà.

Volano:
Del gran duce tartareo
le tue voci, ò Medea, gl'arbitrii legano,
e i numi inferni ai cenni tuoi si piegano.

Pluto le tue voci udì:
in questo cerchio d'or
si racchiude valor
che di Giasone il cor
armerà questo dì.

Medea:
Sì, sì, sì,
vincerà
il mio Rè.
A suo prò
deità
di là giù
pugnerà.
Sì, sì, sì,
vincerà.

Do I call you in vain?
What clamor,
what hissing
prevents my awesome words
from penetrating into the blind chasm?
From the shore
of Cocytus
I summon
all the Furies.
I order you
to my throne.
Why do you still tarry?
Spirits of Tartarus, up, up, up, up!

Chorus of spirits:
Let the walls collapse,
the rocks splinter,
the fortifications crack,
sway and fall,
and soon we will enter
the place where Medea waits.

Volano:
Your words, o Medea, compel
the great King of Tartarus to serve you,
and the gods of the Underworld bend to your
commands.
Pluto has heard your words;
this golden ring
holds within it the valor
that will arm the breast
of Jason today.

Medea:
Yes, yes, yes,
my King
will conquer.
For him the
deity
of the Underworld
will fight.
Yes, yes, yes,
he will conquer.

66b Act II, Scene 11

Scena xi

Besso: *He who has neither silver nor gold   praises poverty and   censures wealth.   Hercules, the grass-*

Chi non hà Ar- gen- ti od o- ri, lo- da la po- ver- ta, bia- sma te- so- ri: Er- co- le ve- do-

widower, far from his   beloved, disconsolate orphan,   chides, chides Jason   for having a lady by his side.

vel- lo, Lun- gi dal- la sua va- ga, or- fa- no scon- so- la- to, sgri- dò, sgri- dò Gia- so- ne ch'ab- bia la Don- na à la- to.

segue il Ritorn:o

Ritornello

Aria

True love,   purest passion   do not lessen   the valour of a   good knight.

Besso: *Love was begotten   by the god of war;   even among arms   woman's beauty is   vaunted;*

D'Af- fet- to sin- cè- ro pu- ris- si- mo ar- dor, di buon Ca- va- lie- ro non sce- ma l'ho-
Dal Dio che guer- reg- gia A- mor nac- que già; fra l'ar- mi pom- peg- gia don- é- sca bel-

A warrior is   scorned   more   for being a pedant   than a lover!
and in the name of the goddess   of war, Bellona, the word "bella" resounds!

nor. V'è più ch'es- ser A- man- te, si dis- di- ce un Guer- rier   far
tà; è guer- rie- ra Bel- lo- na è nel no- me guer- rier   bel-

Alinda: *So many soldiers,   so many!*

da pe- dan- te.   Quan- ti sol- da- ti, ò   quan- ti. Al- le-
la ri- suo- na.

Rejoice,   rejoice,   rejoice,   o amorous women!

grez- za, al- le- grez- za, al- le- grez- za, al- le- grez- za, al- le- grez- za ò Don- ne a- man- ti.

Sinfonia

Alinda: *Welcome   storms,   auspicious gales,   that blow the most   agreeable   wares*

Gra- di- te tem- pe- ste pro- cel- le a- do- ra- te che quà   ne spin- ge- ste le

Besso:
Chi non hà
argenti od ori,
loda la povertà,
biasma i tesori:
Ercole vedovello,
lungi dalla sua vaga,
orfano sconsolato,
sgridò Giason ch'abbia la donna à lato.

D'affetto sincero
purissimo ardor,
di buon cavaliero
non scema l'onor.
V'è più ch'esser Amante,
si disdice a un Guerrier far da pedante.

Dal Dio che guerreggia
Amor nacque già;
fra l'armi pompeggia
donnesca beltà;
e guerriera Bellona,
e nel nome guerrier, bella risuona!

Alinda:
Quanti soldati, ò quanti!
Allegrezza, o donne amanti!

Gradite tempeste,
procelle adorate,
che quà ne spingete
le merci più grate,
per vostra pietate
mia gioia s'avanza;
col vostro tempestar vien l'abbondanza!

Quanti soldati, ò quanti!
Allegrezza, o donne amanti!

Besso:
Per fare in terra un picciol paradiso
ti diè natura, ò bella,
oro al crin, stelle agli occhi, e rose al viso.

Besso:
He who has neither
silver nor gold
praises poverty
and censures wealth.
Hercules, the grass-widower,
far from his beloved,
disconsolate orphan,
chides Jason for having a lady by his side.

True love,
purest passion
do not lessen the honor
of a good knight.
A warrior is scorned
more for being a pedant than a lover!

Love was begotten
by the god of war;
even among arms
woman's beauty is vaunted;
and in the name of the goddess of war,
Bellona, the word "bella" resounds!

Alinda:
So many soldiers, so many!
Rejoice, oh amorous women!

Welcome storms,
auspicious gales,
that blow the most agreeable
wares to our shores!
Thanks to your goodness
my joy is boundless:
as out of your raging comes forth abundance!

So many soldiers, so many!
Rejoice, oh amorous women!

Besso:
To create a little paradise on earth
nature granted, o lovely one,
gold for your tresses, stars for your eyes,
roses for your cheeks.

Alinda:
Per far un uom, tutto robusto e fiero,
ti diè natura in sorte
duro il pel, fosco il fronte, e'l guardo nero.

Besso:
Dimmi, dimmi chi sei,
tú che sì bella sembri agl'occhi miei?

Alinda:
Io sono un'infelice
mal provista d'Amante,
che con affanno inusitato e nuovo
bramo assai, sempre cerco e nulla trovo.

Besso:
Vedimi, e qual io sono,
pur che tu non mi sdegni,
la mia fede, il mio amor tutto ti dono.

Alinda:
Lascia ch'io ben ti guardi;
tu non mi spiaci affé; gli occhi son ladri.

Besso:
Mà i lumi tuoi divini,
se chiami ladri i miei, son assassini!

Alinda:
Esser Amante mio dunque vuoi tu?

Besso:
Rispondo un sì senza pensarci più!

Alinda:
Intendiamoci bene.
Io con modeste voglie per marito ti bramo.

Besso:
Et io per moglie.

Alinda:
Il tuo mestier qual è?

Alinda:
To create a man, vigorous and mettlesome
nature in turn granted you
a hard skin, a dark brow and a black look.

Besso:
Tell me, tell me, who are you
you to whom my eyes seem so fair?

Alinda:
I am an unfortunate creature,
ill-provided with a lover
who, with sudden and unusual anguish,
am stricken with desire, constantly seeking and never
finding.

Besso:
Look at me, see what I am;
if you do not scorn me,
I'll give you all my faith and all my love.

Alinda:
Let me have a good look at you:
in faith, you do not displease me; your eyes are
thieves.

Besso:
If you call my eyes thieves,
then your divine eyes are murderers!

Alinda:
So you want to be my lover?

Besso:
I'll say yes to that without another thought!

Alinda:
Let us understand each other well
With modest desire, I long for you as a husband.

Besso:
And I for you as wife.

Alinda:
What is your trade?

Besso:
Soldato io sono.

Alinda:
Tu soldato? Ah, ah,
oimè questo tuo dir rider mi fa!

Besso:
Perché ridi così?

Alinda:
Tu soldato?

Besso:
Io, sì.

Alinda:
Dov'è il volto sfregiato?
Dov'hai manco un horecchio?
Dov'è un fianco stroppiato?
Dov'è una man recisa?
Oimè, non lo dir più, scoppio di risa!

Besso:
Dunque non ti rassembra
soldato un che intere habbia le membra?

Alinda:
Il buon soldato deve
portar qualche notabil contrasegno,
almen un braccio in pezzi,
un occhio di cristallo ò un piè di legno.
Ma dove vai?

Besso:
Già che così non pare
ch'io sia stato alla guerra,
vado à farmi stroppiare.

Alinda:
No, già che tutto sei, tutto ti voglio.
Ma quanto più ti gradirebbe il Core,
se tù fussi buon musico Cantore!

Besso:
I am a soldier.

Alinda:
You, a soldier? Ha! Ha!
Your words make me laugh!

Besso:
Why do you laugh like that?

Alinda:
You, a soldier?

Besso:
Yes, I am.

Alinda:
Where are the scars on your face?
Where is your missing ear?
Where is your crippled hip?
Where is your chopped up hand?
O my, don't go on, I'll burst with laughter!

Besso:
So, nobody looks like a soldier to you
who still has all his limbs?

Alinda:
A good soldier must bear
some visible mark—
at least an arm cut to shreds,
a glass eye or a wooden leg.
But where are you going now?

Besso:
Since I don't look
as if I've been in the wars,
I'll go and make myself a cripple.

Alinda:
No! Since you are whole, I want you whole.
But how much more you'd charm my heart
if you were a good musician and a singer!

Besso:
Musico? L'arte mia
è'l canto e l'armonia!

Alinda:
Tanto più mi sei grato.
Mà sù quai voci canti, ed in qual tono?

Besso:
Non mi senti al parlar? Soprano io sono.

Alinda:
Soprano?

Besso:
Sì; perché?

Alinda:
Non sei castrato già?

Besso:
Non sono, à fè.

Alinda:
Non più guerra, non più furore:
Due cori Amati,
tra vezzi, e canti
dispensino l'ore.

Besso & Alinda:
Non più guerra, non più, trionfi amore!

Besso:
Non più tromba ò tambur, non più rumore!
In amorose paci
al suono de' baci
rallegris'il core!

Besso & Alinda:
Non più tromba o tamburo, Amore!

FINE DELL'ATTO SECONDO

Besso:
Musician? My art is
singing and harmony.

Alinda:
You please me all the more.
But what is your voice, what register?

Besso:
Can't you hear me speaking? I'm a soprano.

Alinda:
Soprano?

Besso:
Yes. Why?

Alinda:
You are not by chance a castrato?

Besso:
By no means, in faith!

Alinda:
No more war, never, no more fighting,
two loving, loved hearts
will pass the time
in caresses and songs!

Besso & Alinda:
No more war, never again; Love triumphs!

Besso:
No more trumpets or drums, no more frays!
In amorous peace,
to the sound of kisses,
our hearts rejoice!

Besso & Alinda:
No more trumpets or drums! Love!

END OF ACT TWO

66c Act III, Scenes 2-3

Scena ii, Giasone, Medea

Scena iii, Medea, Giasone e Oreste

SCENA II, Medea e Giasone

Medea:
Sotto il tremulo Ciel di queste frondi,
intorno a cui s'aggira
d'aure soavi un odorato nembo,
posa, o mia vita, alla tua vita in grembo.

Giasone:
Mira, mio cor, deh mira,
come nel bel color di queste foglie
speme d'Amor s'accoglie!

Medea:
Vedi, mio cor, deh vedi
qual palesa il candor di questo fiore
la fedeltà d'un core!

Giasone & Medea:
Dunque tra fiori e frondi,
simulacri di fede e della speme,
adorata Medea/adorato Giason, posiamo insieme.

Medea:
Dormi, stanco Giasone,
e del mio Cor, che gl'occhi tuoi rapiro,
sian le palpebre tue cara prigione.

Giasone:
Dormi ch'io dormo, ò bella,
e mentre i sensi miei consegno al sonno,
oggi per te Giason vantar si puote
d'haver l'alma tra l'ombre e in braccio il sole!

Medea:
Mio ben, che sognerai?

Giasone:
I tuoi celesti rai! E tù, mia vita?
Tua bellezza infinita!

Giasone & Medea:
Felicissimo sonno,
che in grembo delle larve al ciel m'invia!
Adoriamoci in sogno, anima mia!

SCENE 2, Medea and Jason

Medea:
Beneath the quivering heaven of these boughs
through which wafts
an odorous mist of sweet breezes,
lie, my love, upon your beloved's bosom.

Jason:
Look, my heart, oh look,
how in the fair color of these leaves
love's hopes are reflected!

Medea:
And look, my heart, oh look,
how in the whiteness of this flower
a heart's constancy is revealed!

Jason & Medea:
Therefore among flowers and boughs,
the images of faith and hope,
adored Medea/adored Jason, let us lie down together.

Medea:
Sleep, weary Jason,
and for my heart, which your eyes have ravished,
let your eyelids be a sweet prison!

Jason:
Sleep, you too, oh beauteous love,
and while I consign my senses to sleep,
today Jason can boast that through you
he has his soul in the shade and the sun in his arms!

Medea:
My love, what will you dream about?

Jason:
Of your heavenly eyes! And you, my life?
Of your infinite beauty!

Jason & Medea:
Most blissful sleep
that raises me to heaven in the bosom of a shade!
Let us adore one another in our dreams, my soul!

SCENA III, Medea, Giasone, e Oreste

Oreste:
"Adoriamoci in sogno, anima mia"?
Gentil discorso è questo,
ma pazzo è ben chi non intende il resto!

Posson questi due cori ben dirsi
innamorati, s'ancora addormentati
se sona avezzi à praticar gl'Amori.
Sto per dir ch'à chius'occhi
l'un con l'altro si mira
e col fiato dell'un l'altro respira.
Qual invidiosa guerra
prova l'anima mia?
Veder due soli addormentati in terra,
ed io qui veglio, e senza compagnia?

Almen per sfogare
sì fiero desio,
addormentare
mi potess'anch'io!

Chè ben sò quanto vaglia
fantastica magia d'un sogno grato
à cacciar fuor lo spirto innamorato.

Non è più bel piacer
quanto in sogno goder
chi si desia!
Gioir in fantasia
con l'adorata Amica
risparmia a quel che sogna
il peccato, la spesa e la fatica!

Curioso amator
sul fabricar ognor
perigli e danni.
Sanz'arte, e senza inganni
à chi dorme è permesso
in grembo alle fantasme
senz'offesa d'altrui saziar l'istesso.

SCENE 3, Medea, Jason, and Oreste

Oreste:
"Let us adore one another in our dreams, my soul?"
A pretty speech, this,
but crazy if you don't understand the rest!

These two hearts can well claim
to be in love, although they sleep,
since they are accustomed to making love.
I can tell that they
see one another with eyes closed
and that they breathe the breath of one another.
What envious assaults
are felt in my soul?
I see two sleeping lovers on the ground
and I watch here without company?

If only I could
go to sleep
and so appease
my wild desire!

I know well how valuable
is the magic fantasy of a pleasant dream
for teasing out the enamored spirit.

There is no greater delight
than to enjoy one's love
in a dream!
To wanton with one's beloved
in one's imagination
saves the dreamer
sin, expense and trouble!

The curious lover,
in creating
dangers and damages all the time,
without art and without deception
to someone who sleeps, is permitted
to satiate himself in bed with with fantasies
without offense to anyone.

66d "E follia" from Act III, Scene 10

Ritor:º da Capo

Delfa:
È follia
fra gl'amori
seminar la gelosia,
per raccoglier alfin rabbie e rancori.
Consolar sol ne può
quel ben che in sen ci sta.
La gioia che passò
in fumo, in ombra, in nulla va.
Chi vuol sbandir dal cor doglia e martello,

lasci amar, ami ogn'un, goda'l più bello!

Non credete
ch'a un'amante
possa trar d'amor la sete
una sola bellezza, un sol sembiante.
Ma s'egli in un sol dì
da doppio amor gode,
fate, o donne, così:
in men d'un'ora gioite con tre!
Chi vuoi goder d'Amor suavi i frutti
un n'accolga, un n'aspetti, aspiri a tutti!

Delfa:
It is madness,
among lovers,
to sow jealousy,
which, in the end, nets anger and rancor.
Comfort comes only from
the love who is in your arms.
Joy that is past
goes up in smoke, shadow, and nothing.
Whoever wishes to banish from her heart pain and throbbing
must be free to love everyone and enjoy the most handsome!

Do not believe
that a single lover
can quench your thirst for love with
a single beauty and a single face.
But if he in a single day
enjoys two lovers,
you, ladies, should do this:
in less than an hour enjoy three!
Whoever wishes to enjoy the sweet fruits of Love
neither gathers nor waits for one, but tries them all!

66e Act III, conclusion

Scena xxi

181

Fine dell'Opera.

SCENA XXI

Egeo:
Io fui che con quel ferro,
di cui conservo la vagina in seno,
o barbaro inumano,
per ferirti a ragion stesi la mano.

Giasone:
Tanto ardisce costui?
E chi ti spinse al tradimento indegno?

Medea:
Fermati! Io lo mandai
per vendicar le mie supposte offense.
Fummo ingannati, Egeo:
senza colpa è Giason, per altro è reo.

Giasone:
Questa innocenza mia a te mi renda.

Medea:
Sono in poter d'Egeo gl'affetti miei.
Rendi ti pur te stesso a chi tu dèi.

Giasone:
A te sempre soggette avrò le voglie.

Medea:
Indiscreto parlar d'un Re ch'ha moglie.

Giasone:
Oh fato averso, ahi sorte!
la vita di costei fù la mia morte!

Isifile:
Infelice, che ascolto?
Non t'affannar, Giasone,
che, se la vita mia
fù, (come ben intesi)
un aborto d'errori
che produce il tuo duolo,
vengo a sacrificarla a tuoi furori.
S'io perivo tra l'acque,
una morte sì breve
forse non appagava i tuoi rigori.

SCENE 21

Aegeus:
I was the one who with this dagger
(the scabbard of which I have upon me),
oh inhuman barbarian,
justly stretched out my hand to kill you.

Jason:
This man dared so much?
And who urged you to this unworthy treachery?

Medea:
Stop! I sent him
to avenge a presumed offence.
We were mistaken, Aegeus:
Toward us Jason is guiltless: his guilt lies elsewhere.

Jason:
This innocence gives me back to you!

Medea:
My affections now belong to Aegeus.
You go back to her to whom you belong.

Jason:
My desires will always be subject to you.

Medea:
What indiscreet speech from a king who has a wife!

Jason:
Oh adverse fate, oh, what misfortune!
Her life was my death!

Hypsipyle:
Unhappy me, what do I hear?
But do not vex yourself, Jason,
for if my life
was (as I have clearly understood)
the unwelcome result of a mistake,
that has caused you this suffering,
I come to sacrifice it to your fury.
If I had perished in the water,
so quick a death
might not have appeased your wrath.

Mà se viva son io,
rallegrati, o crudele,
già che potrai con replicate morti
sfogar del fiero cor l'empio desio!
Sì sì, tiranno mio,
ferisci à parte à parte
queste membra abborrite!
Sbranami à poco a poco
queste carni infelici!
Anatomizza il seno!
Straziami a tuo piacere!
Martirizami i sensi,
e 'l mio lento morire
prolunghi a me 'l tormento, a te 'l giore.
Mà se d'esser marito
l'adorate memorie alfin perdesti,
fa ch'il nome di Padre
frà le tue crudeltadi intatto resti!
Non ti scordar, Giason, che padre sei
e che son di te parte i parti miei!
Se legge di natura
obliga à gl'elementi anche le fiere,
fà che mano pietosa
gli somministri almen vitto mendico,
e non soffrir ch'i tuoi scettrati figli,
per la fame languenti
spirin l'alme innocenti.
Regina, Egeo, amici,
supplicate per me questo crudele,
che nel ferirmi lasci
queste mammelle da' suoi colpi intatte,
acciò nutrisca almeno i figli miei
del morto sen materno un freddo latte!
Pregatelo pietosi
che quegl'Angel'i infanti
assistino a i martiri
della madre tradita,
e che ad ogni ferita
che imprimerà nel mio pudico petto
bevino quelli il sangue mio stillante,
acciò ch'ei trapassando
nelle lor pure vene in lor s'incarni,
onde il lor seno in qualche parte sia
tomba innocente all'innocenza mia!
A dio terra, a dio sole,
a dio Regina amica! Amico a dio!

But since I live,
rejoice, o cruel wretch!
For now with repeated deaths
you may vent your savage heart's wicked desires!
Yes, yes, my tyrant,
hack them apart,
these abhorred limbs!
Rend to pieces, bit by bit,
this unhappy flesh!
Dissect my breast!
Lacerate me at your pleasure!
Torture my senses
and let my slow death
prolong my torment and your enjoyment!
But if you have already lost
the loving memory of being a husband,
let the title of father
remain unsullied by your cruelties!
Do not forget, Jason, that you are a father
and that my children are a part of you!
If the law of Nature
compels even wild beasts to feed them,
let a merciful hand
provide them at least with a beggar's nourishment,
and do not permit that your sons, born to the scepter,
languishing with hunger,
relinquish their innocent souls.
Queen, Aegeus, friends,
beseech this cruel one on my behalf
that in wounding me he leave
my breasts untouched by his blows,
so that my sons may at least
feed on the cold milk of their dead mother!
Mercifully beg him
that these angelic children
witness the martyrdom
of their betrayed mother,
and that with every blow
that marks my chaste breast,
they may drink the blood flowing from me,
so that in passing
into their pure veins it shall become part of their flesh,
and thus their breasts will become in part
the innocent tomb of my innocence!
Farewell earth, farewell sun,
farewell queenly friend! Friends, farewell!

A dio scettri, a dio patria, adio mia prole!
Sciolta la madre vostra
dal suo terrestre velo
attenderà di rivedervi in Cielo.
Venite, cari pegni,

temp'è ch'io vi consegni
all'adorato mostro
ch'è carnefice mio e Padre vostro.
Figli, v'attendo e moro.
E te Giason, ben ch'homicida, adoro.

Giasone:
Non ho più core in petto.
Scoppia l'alma nel seno.
Taci, Isifile, taci,
non mi confonder più, vinto son io.
Figli, moglie, cor mio!
Trà le colpe avvilito,
da Isifile difeso,
chieder pietà non oso,
Padre inumano e traditor Marito.
Ah da te, mia tradita,
impetrino da me perdono e pace
il mio pianto, il mio duol, gl'amplessi, i baci.
Egeo, Medea, godete
vostri felici ardori,
e mentr'in ogni cor la gioia abbonda,
un contento improvviso
le trascorse vicende
in mar d'amico oblio chiuda e confonda.
Vinto, vinto son io!
figli, moglie, cor mio!

Isifile:
Mio smarrito tesoro,
s'io ti riacquisto, oh Dio,
non ho più che bramare,
e son le mie dolcezze,
quanto stentate più, tanto più care!

Farewell scepters, farewell my country, farewell my children! Released from the mortal coils,
your mother
will wait to see you again in heaven.
Come you, come, my children, dear tokens of my love,
the time has come for me to deliver you
to the beloved monster,
my executioner and your father.
Children, I await you, and I die.
And you, Jason, although my murderer, I love you.

Jason:
I no longer have a heart in my breast.
My soul bursts within my bosom.
Silence, Hypsipyle, o silence,
Shame me no more; I am vanquished.
My children, my wife, my heart!
Humbled by these blows,
defended by Hypsipyle herself
I do not dare to cry for mercy,
inhuman father and faithless husband that I am.
Ah, may my tears, my sorrow, my embraces and kisses
implore my forgiveness and peace
from you whom I have betrayed.
Aegeus, Medea, rejoice
in your happy loves,
and while joy abounds in every heart,
may an unforeseen happiness
swallow up and drown in a sea of kindly oblivion
all that has happened.
I am vanquished, vanquished,
my children, my wife, my heart!

Hypsipyle:
My lost treasure,
if I recover you, o God!
I have nothing more to desire,
and my bliss is all the more precious
for having been so hard-won.

Isifile & Giasone:
Quante son le mie gioie
tante stille il mar non ha.
Quante son le mie gioie
tante stelle il ciel non ha.
Mia dolcezza./Mia bellezza.
Nel tuo seno morire mi sento già,
ch'a tanto gioire
un'alma sola resister non sa.

Isifile & Medea:
Godi, Medea/Isifile, godi,
stringa amor, Egeo/Giasone, suoi dolci nodi!

Jason & Hypsipyle:
My joy is even greater
than the drops in the ocean.
My joy is even greater
than the stars in the sky.
My sweet love/My fair love,
upon your breast I feel myself languishing,
for so much rapture
cannot be borne by a single soul.

Hypsipyle & Medea:
Rejoice, Medea/Hypsipyle, rejoice!
Let love with Aegeus/Jason tie his sweet knots!

Stop your course, o Fortune, teach me desire. Hold still your inconstant wheel.

Fis-sa il chio-do, o For-ti-na. In-se-gna-mi a bra-mar o tie-ni im-mo-ta Tu vo-lu-bi-le

If you are enamored of me, royal beauty, my soul desires no more.

ro-ta. Se di me s'in-va-ghì re-gia bel-tà, Più de-si-ar non sa L'al-ma che tut-te in

It has all joys in one. Stop your course, o Fortune.

sè le gio-ie a-du-na. Fis-sa il chio-do, o For-tu-na.

Thus I have enough. I aspire to nothing better. I went to sleep a beggar and awoke a king.

Co-sì mi ba-sta non a-spi-ro a me-glio, M'ad-dor-men-tai men-di-co e re mi sve-glio.

Fine
dell'atto

SCENA XVII, Orontea sola

Orontea:
Intorno all'idol mio,
Spirate, pur spirate
Aure soavi e grate,
E nelle guance elette
Baciate lo per me, cortesi aurette.
Al mio ben che riposa
Su l'ali della quiete
Grati sogni assistete,
E'l mio racchiuso ardore
Svelateli per me, larve d'amore.
Ohirnè, non son più mia!
Se mi sprezza Alidoro
Sarà la vita mia preda di morte.
Questo diadema d'oro
Ch'io ti pongo sui crine.
Questo scettro real nacque per tè.
Tu sei l'anima mia, tu sei mio re.
O Dio, chi vide mai
Più bella maestà, più bel regnante?
Divino è quel sembiante,
Innamorano il ciel quei chiusi rai,
Più bella maestà, chi vide mai?
Ma nel mio cor sepolto
Non vò'tener lo stral, che mi ferì.
Una regina amante
Non vuol penar, non vuol morir così.
Leggi, o mio caro,
In negre note i miei sinceri amori,
In brevi accenti immensità d'ardori.
Dormi, ben mio,
Per te veglia Orontea; mia vita, addio.

SCENE 17, Orontea alone

Orontea:
Around about my idol
waft, oh waft,
ye breezes soft and kind,
and his lovely cheeks
kiss for me, gentle winds.
Grant my love who rests
upon the wings of peace
sweet dreams,
and my secret ardor
reveal to him for me, spirits of love.
Alas, I no longer possess myself;
if Alidoro disdains me,
my life will be a prey to death.
This golden diadem
I place upon your head,
this royal sceptre, both were born for you.
You are my soul, you are my king.
Oh gods, who has ever seen
fairer majesty, a fairer ruler!
This countenance is divine.
His closed eyes enamour heaven.
Who has ever seen fairer majesty?
But buried in my heart
I will not keep the dart that wounded me.
An amorous Queen
will not suffer, will not die like this.
So read, read, my dearest,
in black letters my true love,
in brief words the immensity of my passion.
Sleep, sleep, my love:
Orontea watches over you. My life, farewell.

SCENA XVIII

Alidoro:
Qual profondo letargo
I sensi miei legò?
Dove son io, chi mi svegliò?
Chi mi diè questo scettro e questa carta?
Da qual peso
Le tempie sento gravarmi? Ohimè,
Chi m'ingemmò le chiome, e che sarà?
Così occulti misteri
Questa carta ridir forse saprà.
"Alidoro, t'adoro;
Silandra e mia rivale;
Vincon regio decoro
Amore e gelosia, coppia fatale;
Vincon le tue bellezze un cor invitto.
Sarai mia sposo, e regnator d'Egitto.
All'adorato ben che l'invaghì
La gelosa Orontea scrisse così."
Care note amorose,
Che palesate a me regia pietade;
Nel sacrario del core
Vi deposito umil note d'amore.
Resta in pace, Silandra,
Aspira al maggior segno il mio desire.
La mia brama è cangiata,
Non voglia ingelosir sposa scettrata.
Fu l'ardor ch'io provai
Rogo di morte, e fu'l mio cor fenice;
Incenerito ei giaque:
Morto a Silandra, ad Orontea rinacque.
Fissa il chiodo, o Fortuna.
Insegnami a bramai o tieni immota
Tua volubile rota.
Se di me s'invaghi regia beltà,
Più desiar non sà
L'alma che tutte in sè le gioie aduna.
Fissa il chiodo, o Fortuna.
Così mi basta non aspiro a meglio,
M'addormentai mendico e rè mi sveglio.

SCENE 18

Alidoro:
What deep lethargy
imprisoned my senses?
Where am I, who has awakened me?
Who gave me this sceptre and this letter?
What weight do I feel
pressing on my temples? Alas!
Who has adorned my brow? What is this?
This paper perhaps will explain
these strange mysteries.
"Alidoro, I adore you,
Silandra is my rival:
My royal splendor has been vanquished
by love and jealousy (fatal pair).
Your beauty has conquered my unvanquished heart.
You will be my husband and King of Egypt.
To the adored beloved who has won her,
the jealous Orontea has written this."
Dear words of love
that reveal to me the royal mercy,
in the sanctuary of my heart
be laid, humble words of love.
Live in peace, Silandra,
my will aspires to higher places.
My demands have changed;
do not make a crowned wife jealous.
The ardor I felt
was a funeral pyre, my heart is its Phoenix.
It lies reduced to ashes.
Dead to Silandra, it is reborn to Orontea.
Stop your course, oh Fortune,
teach me desire, hold still
your inconstant wheel.
If you are enamored of me, royal beauty,
my soul desires no more;
It has all joys in one.
Stop your course, o Fortune.
Thus I have enough, I aspire to nothing better.
I went to sleep a beggar and awoke a king.

Dimmi Amor, che fia di me?	Tell me, Cupid, what will become of me
In si cruda servitù	In such cruel bondage,
Se resister non può più	if my faith cannot longer endure
Combattuta la mia fè.	under attack?

69 BARBARA STROZZI, *L'Eraclito amoroso* (1651)

from her *Cantate, ariette e duetti . . . opera seconda*

(Venice, 1651)

Udite amanti la cagione, o Dio,
ch'a lagrimar mi porta:
nell'adorato e bello idolo mio,
che sì fido credei, la fede è morta.

Vaghezza ho sol di piangere,
mi pasco sol di lagrime,
il duolo è mia delizia
e son miei gioie i gemiti.
Ogni martire aggradami,
ogni dolor dilettami,
i singulti mi sanano,
i sospir mi consolano.

Ma se la fede negami
quell'incostante e perfido,
almen fede serbatemi
sino alla morte, o lagrime!
Ogni tristezza assalgami,
ogni cordoglio eternisi,
tanto ogni male affligami
che m'uccida e sotterrimi.

Hear, you lovers, the reason, oh God,
that brings me to tears:
in my adored and beautiful idol,
believed by me to be so true, faith is dead.

Weeping is my only pastime,
tears are my only food,
grief is my delight,
and my joys are sighs.
Every martyrdom pleases me,
every pain delights me,
sobs heal me,
sighs console me.

But if my inconstant and perfidious friend
denies me lover's faith,
then you, at least, oh tears,
be true to me unto death!
May every sadness befall me,
may every sorrow be eternal,
may every evil afflict me
to kill me and bury me!

70 ANTONIO CESTI, *Languia già l'alba* (ca. 1660)

from I:Rvat, Barb. Lat. 4156

Languia già l'alba, e la ridente Aurora
spargendo innanzi al Sole
odorifera prole
de' begli occhi di Flora,
vaga del suo ritorno,
formava in ciel cuna di rose al giorno.
Quand'ecco all'improviso
davanti agli occhi miei
lieta e placida in viso
parmi veder colei ch'il sen m'aprì,
e mentre al suo bel volto
fisso le luci, ascolto
che mi parla così:

Already dawn was languishing, and the smiling Aurora,
scattering before the sun
the fragrant progeny
of Flora's beautiful eyes,
longing for its return,
was weaving, in the sky, a cradle of roses for the day.
When, behold, suddenly
before my eyes,
joyful and placid in countenance,
I seemed to see her who wounded my heart.
And while upon her beautiful face
I fixed my eyes, I heard
her speak to me in this way:

Non mi conosci, no?
Apri i lumi, osserva e godi,
mira et odi
chi suo ben, suo cor t'appella,
mira pur s'io pur son quella
che teco più festiva un dì sarò.
Non mi conosci, no?

You do not know me, do you?
Open your eyes, see and enjoy;
look at and listen to
her who calls you her dear, her heart;
see if I am she
who, more joyous, one day will be with you.
You do not know me, do you?

Sì, ch'io son quella, sì!
Non temer, bell'idol mio,
son quell'io che talor tua gloria chiami,
son colei che tanto brami
colei che vien per adorarti quì.
Si, ch'io son quella, si!

Yes, I am she, yes!
Fear not, my beautiful idol,
I am she whom at times you call your glory,
I am she for whom you long so much,
she who comes to adore you here.
Yes, I am she, yes!

Ed ecco in quell'istante,
mentr'io la seguo invano,
porgendomi la mano
per gli occhi fiammeggiò rai di contento
e replicando in suon allegro e pio
un dolcissimo addio,
tacque, rise, disparve in un momento.
Allor mi desto, e chiaro
già rimirando il bel nascente lume,
abbandono le piume.
Indi al suon che lasciaro
le voci del mio cor centro mio core
congiungo il canto e chi n'è cause, Amore:

And behold, in that instant
when I followed her in vain,
taking my hand
she beamed rays of contentment from her eyes.
And replying, in a tone happy and pious,
with a most sweet farewell,
she fell silent, smiled, and disappeared in an instant.
How I awaken and understand: already seeing
the brightness of the beautiful dawning light,
I abandon my bed.
Then, to the accompaniment that
the voices of my heart left within my heart,
I join the melody and that which is the cause of it:
love.

Mi dipinge amabil Sorte
vision così gradita,
il germano della Morte
mi congiunge alla mia vita.
E tu solo per mio duolo
nasci, o Febo, acciò che morto
io compianga il mio conforto.
Ah, se ben da te si sgombra
ogni nube, o pur ogn'ombra,
dirti già non poss'io
l'auriga, il nume, il dio ch'il giorno adduce
se sparisce al tuo lume ogni mia luce.

Kindly Fate paints for me
a lovely vision;
the brother of Death
joins me to my life.
And you alone, to my sorrow,
are born, oh Phoebus, so that, dead,
I may lament my comfort.
Ah, even though you sweep away
every cloud or every shadow,
I cannot yet call you
the charioteer, the spirit, the god who brings the day
if, with your light, all my light vanishes.

71 MARCO MARAZZOLI, *San Tomaso* (ca. 1650), conclusion to Part 1

from I:Bc, Q 43

Credi, credi, o Tomaso!
Beato è chi non vede
ma solo spera e crede.

Believe, believe, oh Thomas!
Blessed is he that sees not,
but only hopes and believes.

Apostolo:
Qual virtù rimirò il pietoso
Signor ch'apostolico Trono
à noi donò?
Non merto, non tesor
mà sol candida fè
di si sublime honor degni ci fè.

An Apostle:
Which virtue was seen by the good Lord,
who has given us
the apostolic throne?
Not merit, not riches,
but only pure faith made us
worthy of such a sublime honor.

Apostoli:
Credi, credi, ó Tomaso!
Beato è chi non vede
mà solo spera e crede.

Apostles:
Believe, believe, oh Thomas!
Blessed is he that sees not,
but only hopes and believes.

Apostolo:
Marta ha fede,
e prieghi porgere
mai non cessa al Ré sovrano.
Onde vede poi risorgere
il sepolto suo Germano.

An Apostle:
Martha has faith,
and prayers pouring forth
without end to the King omnipotent.
That is why she then saw the resurrection
of her buried brother.

Apostolo:
Di pregar mai non si satia
la dolenta Cananea,
che sua figlia egra giacea
egli otten celesti gratia.

An Apostle:
Of praying she never had enough,
the sorrowful Canaanite,
whose daughter lay ill.
He gave her heavenly grace.

Pietro:
Reo ch'in croce hebbe fiducia
degno fù del Regno eterno;
l'altro poi nel cieco Inferno
tormentato ogn'hor si cruccia.

Peter:
The thief who on the cross had faith
was held worthy of the eternal Kingdom.
The other in the gloomy inferno
is forever racked by torments.

Apostoli:
Credi, credi, ó Tomaso!
Beate è chi non vede
mà solo spera e crede.

Apostles:
Believe, believe, oh Thomas!
Blessed is he that sees not,
but only hopes and believes.

Pietro:
Dalla turba seguace
volle un giorno il Signore
udir qual fosse
il Figliolo dell'huom Messia verace.
Vi fò chi disse Elia,
altri Giovanni ed altri Geremia.
Io costante affermai
con fè sincera
che gli del vero Dio figlio sol era.
Ond'ei rispose:
"E tu quel Pietro sei della mia Chiesa,
e fondamento, e pietra."
Così mia fè m'impetra le chiavi ancor
del gran Monarca eterno
d'aprir il Ciel e riserrar l'Inferno.

Peter:
From the host of his disciples
the Lord one day wished
to hear which
son of man might be the true Messiah.
Some said "Elijah," others
"John," yet others "Jeremiah."
I loyally asserted
with sincere faith
that he was the only son of the Living God.
Whereupon he answered:
"And you are Peter,
the rock and the foundation of my church."
Thus my belief granted me, with the keys
of the great, eternal Monarch, the power
to open the Heavens and to lock up hell.

from I:MOe, Mus. f. 1136

Erodiade la Figlia:
Aria:
Vaghe Ninfe del Giordano
che movete al ballo il piè
deh, mi dite
se gioite
dentro l'alma al par di me?
Anco in Ciel le stelle tremule
vezzosette ogn'ora danzano,
ma per questo non avanzano
il mio cor, di cui son' emule.

Consigliere:
Giorno sì lieto in vero
in cui del tuo natale
la memoria si venera, ed honora,
haver non potea mai più bell'Aurora.

Aria:
Anco il sol, fuor dell'usato
cinto il sen di rai lucenti,
par che dica a noi viventi:
Quest'è il di ch'Erode è nato!

Herode:
O di questi occhi miei luce più chiara,
Erodiade, cara,
chiedi pur ciò che vuoi,
che sicure saran le tue richieste.

Figlia:
Signor, da tua bontade altro non bramo
che sol benigno inverso me si giri:
patrimonio che basta ai miei desiri.

Herode:
Con sì dolci maniere
talmente usurpi degli affetti il trono
che l'offerirti in dono
stimo vil la metà anco del regno.
Vanne, ritorna, e chiedi,
che magnanimo re che i servi honora
è superiore alle dimande ancora.

Herodias, the Daughter:
Aria:
Charming nymphs of the Jordan,
who move your feet in dance
oh, tell me,
do you rejoice
in your souls as I do?
In the heavens, too, the twinkling stars
charmingly dance constantly,
but in this they cannot surpass
my heart, which they would emulate.

Counselor:
A day so happy indeed,
in which we venerate and honor
the memory of your birth
could surely have no finer dawn.

Aria:
Even the sun, more than usual,
is wreathed with shining rays,
as if to say to us mortals:
This is the day on which Herod was born.

Herod:
Oh brightest light of my eyes,
dear Herodias,
ask for anything you want,
for your request will he granted.

Daughter:
Sir, of your generosity I desire nothing
except that it remain well-disposed toward me:
that inheritance is all I desire.

Herod:
With such sweet manners
do you usurp the affection of the throne,
so that to offer you
a mere half my kingdom seems miserly.
Go then, return, and ask
that a generous king who honors his servants
surpasses even their wishes.

Santo:
Godete pur, godete
in grembo del piacere, in braccio ai sensi,
ciechi mortali, ardete, a vana deità vittime, e incensi!

Aria:
Io, per me, no cangerei
così ferme ho le mie voglie,
l'altrui felicità con le mie doglie.
Graditi tormenti
che l'alma agitate
con aspro rigor,
voi siete contenti
che gioia portate a questo mio cor.
Io, per me, non cangerei,
sì costante è il mio desio,
con l'altrui libertade il carcer mio.

Herodiade, la Madre:
Figlia, se un gran tesoro
brami di conseguir dal regio affetto
chiedi sol di Battista il teschio altero—
dono maggior di qualsi voglia impero:
che se cade recisa
la di lui lingua al suolo
trofeo riman delle nostr'armi Herode,
e chi d'un re trionfa il regno gode.

Figlia:
Regnator glorioso,
di tue promesse il lusinghiero invito
vorrei; ch'ossequioso
sembrasse il mio desire, e non ardito,
che con egual timore
stassi se tace o pur se parla il core.

Herode:
Parla; la fede mia l'impegno e giuro
che dal poter d'Augusto
tutto quel che domande impetra il giusto.

Figlia:
Bramo sol che Battista . . .

Herode:
Habbi la libertà.

Figlia:
Bramo. ma temo . . .

The Saint:
Rejoice, then, rejoice
in pleasure's bosom, in the senses' embrace,
blind mortals, and burn, for a vain deity, victims and
incense.

Aria:
I, for my part, would not exchange,
so firm are my wishes,
the happiness of others for my sorrow.
Welcome torments
that agitate my soul
with harsh rigor,
you are the pleasures
that bring joy to my heart.
I, for my part, would not exchange,
so firm are my wishes,
the happiness of others for my sorrow.

Herodias, the Mother:
Daughter, if a great treasure
you wish to obtain from the king's affection,
then ask only for the Baptist's proud head:
a greater gift than any empire,
for if it is cut off,
his tongue falls to the ground,
and Herod remains as our weapons' trophy,
and he who wins the king enjoys his kingdom.

Daughter:
Glorious ruler,
the attractive offer of your promises
I wish to accept;
may my wish seem not presumptuous,
for I fear equally
remaining silent or allowing my heart to speak.

King Herod:
Speak! I give you my word and swear
that by the power of Augustus
all that you request will be judged fitting.

Daughter:
I ask only that the Baptist . . .

King Herod:
Speak freely.

Daughter:
I want to, but I fear . . .

Herode:
Deh, rompi ogni dimora;
esponi il tuo desio.

Figlia:
Bramo che mora.

Herode:
Ahi, troppo brami; e al qual cagione il chiedi?
Sento dure contese
di pietà nel mio core.

Figlia:
Egli t'offese.

Herode:
Ma s'ei fosse innocente?

Figlia:
Reo si fà
chi di un re provocò la deità.

Herode e la Figlia, à2:
Nel seren de' tuoi/miei contenti
da più venti
combattuta è la mia/tua nave:
sdegno, amor, pietade, ed ira
mal/mi s'aggira
nel tuo/entr'il sen dolente e grave.

Figlia:
Deh, che più tardi a consolar la speme
di questo afflitto core
che più viver non può, se vive ancora
chi le sue grazie atterra, e discolora!
Il seren della fronte obblia l'avorio e l'ostro
solo in udir, solo in mirar quel mostro.

Aria:
Queste lagrime, e sospiri
che tu miri
braman solo, o mio gran re,
braman pur poca mercè.

Herode:
In questa degli affetti
dubbia tempesta e fiera,
vinse la crudeltà. Battista pera.

King Herod:
Come, abandon your misgivings;
explain your desire.

Daughter:
I want him to perish.

King Herod:
Ah, you ask too much! And why this request?
I feel strong resistance
and pity in my heart.

Daughter:
He offends you.

King Herod:
But what if he were innocent?

Daughter:
He makes himself guilty
who provokes the deity of a king.

Herod and his daughter, duet:
Beneath the serene sky of your/my contentment
by many winds
your/my ship is assailed:
anger and love, pity and wrath
chase one another
in your/my sad and solemn breast.

Daughter:
Oh, since you hesitate to fulfil the hope
of this afflicted heart,
it cannot live any longer, if he still lives
who debases and discolors its grace!
The serenity of my brow loses its ivory and rose
merely in hearing or seeing that monster.

Aria:
These tears and sighs
you see before you
desire only, oh great king,
desire only a little mercy.

Herod:
In this uncertain and wild
tempest of my feelings
cruelty is victorious. Let the Baptist perish!

73 GIACOMO CARISSIMI, *Suscitavit Dominus* (1665)

from *Scelta de' motetti da cantarsi a due e tre voci composti in musica da diversi eccellentissimi autori romani* (Rome, 1665)

Suscitavit Dominus super Babilonem	Over Babylon and its dwellers
et super habitatores eius	the Lord called up
quasi ventum pestilentem	a pestilential wind
misit ventilatores et ventilabunt	he sent judges and they passed judgment
et demolientur eam.	and they destroyed the city.
Fugite, fugite gentes, fugite populi,	Flee, people flee, people flee,
fugite de medio Babilonis	flee from the midst of Babylon
et salvet unusquisque animam suam.	and let each person save his soul.
Super muros eius levate signum	Above the walls raise the ensign,
augete custodiam, properate insidias,	increase the guard, prepare the defense,
acuite saggittas, implete pharetras	sharpen your arrows, fill your quivers,
quia ultia Domini est;	for this is the vengeance of the Lord;
mens eius est ut perdat eam	his thought is to destroy
et ponat urbem fortem in ruinam.	and to lay waste the city
Fugite, fugite gentes, fugite populi,	Flee, people flee, people flee,
fugite de media Babilonis	flee from the midst of Babylon
et salvet unusquisque animam suam.	and let each person save his soul.
Infelix Babilon, quae habitas super acquas,	Wretched Babylon that lives by abundant water,
multas locuplex in thesauris,	rich in treasure;
venit finis tuus, venit interitus tuus,	your end is come, your fate is come,
venit dies praecisionis tuae.	your day of judgment is nigh.
Cessaverunt fortes tui a praelio,	Your strongest men faltered in battle,
habitaverunt in praesidiis	they dwelt in armed camps;
devoratum est robut eorum	devoured is their valor,
incensa sunt tabernacula tua.	burnt are your tabernacles,
Fugite, fugite gentes, fugite populi,	Flee, people flee, people flee,
fugite de medio Babilonis	flee from the midst of Babylon
et salvet unusquisque animam suam.	and let each man save his soul.

74 ISABELLA LEONARDA, *Ave suavis dilectio* (1676)

from her *Motteti a voce sola, parte con istromenti, e parte senza*

. . . opera sesta (Venice, 1676)

Ave suavis dilectio.	Hail, sweet love.
Salve caritatis repletio.	Greetings, fullness of charity.
O cibus cibans, o mensa immensa,	Oh nourishing food, oh immense banquet,
de te bibere vivere est,	to drink of thee is to live,
de te pasci nasci est.	to eat of thee is to be born.
Salve lumen animarum.	Greetings, light of our souls.
Ave flumen gratiarum.	Hail, river of grace.
Si sitio tu satias,	If I thirst, thou quenchest.
si esurio tu resicis.	If I hunger, thou satest,
O! amoris misterium,	oh mystery of love,
peccatoris refrigerium.	refuge of sinners.
In Te salus,	In Thee is salvation,
in Te vita,	in Thee is life,
in Te totus paradisus.	in Thee is all of Paradise.
De pane gloria,	From bread cometh glory,
de pane de vino divinitas.	from bread and from wine divinity,
de morte vita!	from death, life!
O pro mortalibus vitalis mors,	For mortals, life through death,
vere fidelibus.	for the truly faithful.
O qualis fors!	Oh, what fortune!

75 JEAN-BAPTISTE LULLY, *Airs pour le carrousel de monseigneur*, LWV 72 (1686)

from F:V, Ms. mus. 186; and I:Pn, Fonds du Conservatoire,

Rés F 671

Prelude du Carousel de la Grande Escurie: Concert de trompettes, hautbois et timballes

Gavotte pour les trompettes et hautbois

76 LOUIS COUPERIN, *Tombeau de M. de Blancrocher* (ca. 1652)

from F;Pn, Rés.Vm[7] 674–5

77 LOUIS COUPERIN, Prélude (ca. 1657)

from F;Pn, Rés.Vm⁷ 674–5

78 JEAN DE SAINTE-COLOMBE, *Concert "Le tendre"* (ca. 1670)

from F:Pn, Département de la Musique, Réserve

Vma ms. 866

79 HENRY DU MONT, *Tristitia vestra* (1652)

from his *Cantica sacra . . . liber primus* (Paris, 1652)

Tristitia vestra, alleluya,
convertetur in gaudium: alleluya.
Mundus autem gaudebit,
vos vero contristabimini,
sed tristitia vestra
convertetur in gaudium: alleluya.

Your sadness, alleluia,
will be changed to rejoicing, alleluia.
The world will rejoice,
but you shall be sorrowful,
but your sorrow
will be changed into rejoicing, alleluia.

80 JEAN-BAPTISTE LULLY, *Alceste, ou le triomphe d'Alcide*, LWV 50 (1674), Act I

from F:V, Ms mus 95, and other sources, with content

chosen to correspond with the currently available

commercial recording

Scène troisième
STRATON, LYCHAS

231

Scène cinquième

LICOMÈDE, STRATON, CÉPHISE

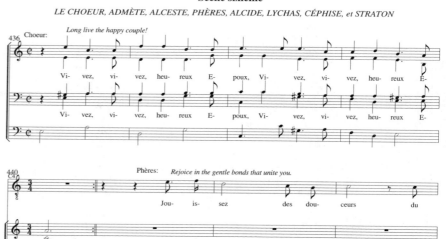

Scène sixième

LE CHOEUR, ADMÈTE, ALCESTE, PHÈRES, ALCIDE, LYCHAS, CÉPHISE, et STRATON

Scène septième

Des nymphes de la Mer, et des Tritons, viennent faire une Feste Marine, où se meslent des Matelots, et des Pescheurs.
Sea Nymphs and Tritons enter to take part in a sea fete in which mingle mariners and fishermen.

Céphise vestue en Nymphe de la Mer, chante au milieu des Divinitez Marines qui lui repondent.
Cephise dressed as a Sea Nymph sings in the midst of the Sea Divinities who answer her.

Licomède conduit Alceste dans son vaisseau, Straton y mène Céphise, et dans le temps qu'Admète et Alcide y veulent passer, le Pont s'enfonce dans la Mer.

Lycomedes leads Alcestis onto his ship. Straton escorts Cephise, and just as Admetus and Alcides are about to embark, the bridge crumbles into the Sea.

Scène huitième

THÉTIS, ADMETE, ALCIDE

Thétis rentre dans la Mer, et les Aquilons excitent une tempeste qui agite les Vaisseaux qui s'efforcent de poursuivre Licomède.

Thetis returns into the sea and the Aquilons rage a tempest that rocks the ships that try to pursue Lycomedes

Les Vents
Entrée des Aquilons

Scène neuvième

EOLE, LES AQUILONS, LES ZEPHIRS

ACTE PREMIER

La Sçene est dans la Ville d'Yolcos en Thessalie. Le Theatre represente un Port de Mer, ou l'on void un grand Vaisseau orné et preparé pour une Feste galante au milieu de plusieurs Vaisseaux de guerre.

SCENE PREMIERE.
Le choeur des Thessaliens, Alcide, Lychas.

Le choeur:
Vivez, vivez, heureux Espoux.

Lychas:
Vostre Amy le plus cher espouze la Princesse
La plus charmante de la Grece,
Lorsque chacun les suit, Seigneur, les fuyez-vous?

Le choeur:
Vivez, vivez, heureux Espoux.

Lychas:
Vous paroissez troublé des cris qui retentissent?
Quand deux heureux Amants s'unissent
Le Choeur du grand Alcide en serait-il jaloux?

Le choeur:
Vivez, vivez, heureux Espoux.

Lychas:
Seigneur, vous soupirez, et gardez le silence?

Alcide:
Ah Lychas, laisse moy partir en diligence.

Lychas:
Quoy dés ce mesme jour presser vostre départ?

ACT I

The scene is in the city of Iolcos in Thessaly. The theater represents a seaport in which one can see a large ship decorated and prepared for a wedding celebration in the middle of several warships.

SCENE 1
Chorus of Thessalians, Alcides, Lychas

Chorus:
Long live the happy couple!

Lychas:
Your dearest friend is marrying a princess,
the most charming in Greece.
While everyone follows them, sir, will you avoid them?

Chorus:
Long live the happy couple!

Lychas:
You seem troubled by all of this rejoicing.
When two happy lovers are united,
is the heart of the great Alcides jealous?

Chorus:
Long live the happy couple!

Lychas:
My Lord, do you sigh and remain silent?

Alcides:
Ah Lychas, let me leave at once.

Lychas:
What? On this very day hasten your departure?

Alcide:
J'auray beau me presser je partiray trop tard.
Ce n'est point avec toy que je pretens me taire;
Alceste est trop aimable, elle a trop sçeu me plaire;
Un autre en est aimé, rien ne flatte mes voeux,
C'en est fait, Admète l'espouze,
Et c'est dans ce moment qu'on les unit tous deux.
Ah qu'une âme jalouse
Esprouve un tourment rigoureux!
J'ay peine à l'exprimer moy-mesme:
Figure toy, si tu le peux,
Qu'elle est l'horreur extreme
De voir ce que l'on aime
Au pouvoir d'un Rival heureux.

Lychas:
L'amour est-il plus fort qu'un HEROS indomptable?
L'Univers n'a point eu de Monstre redoutable
Que vous n'ayez pu surmonter.

Alcide:
Eh crois-tu que l'Amour soit moins à redouter?
Le plus grand Coeur a sa foiblesse.
Je ne puis me sauver de l'ardeur qui me presse
Qu'en quittant ce fatal Sejour:
Contre d'aimables charmes
La Valeur est sans armes,
Et ce n'est qu'en fuyant qu'on peut vaincre l'Amour.

Lychas:
Vous devez vous torcer, au moins, à voir la Feste
Qui déja dans ce Port vous paroist toute preste.
Vostre fuite à present feroit un trop grand bruit;

Ditterez jusques à la nuit.

Alcides:
Well might you urge me to leave later.
It is not with you that I think to tarry.
Alceste is too lovely; she pleases me too much.
But she loves another, there is not hope for me.
It is decided, she will marry Admetus,
and the ceremony is taking place right now.
Ah! How a jealous soul
feels harsh torment!
I can hardly express it myself.
Imagine, if you can,
how extremely horrible it is
to see the one you love
in the hands of a lucky rival.

Lychas:
Is Love stronger than an invincible HERO?
The universe has yet to harbor a formidable monster
that you have been unable to subdue.

Alcides:
Do you believe that Love is less to be feared?
The greatest heart has its weakness.
I can only escape the passion that oppresses me.
by quitting this fatal visit:
Against adorable charms
courage is without allies,
and it is only in fleeing it that Love may be conquered.

Lychas:
You must at least promise to see the festivities,
which, as you see, have already begun in the harbor.
Your immediate departure would create too much noise.
Wait until night.

Alcide:
Ah Lychas! quelle nuit! ah quelle nuit funeste!

Lychas:
Tout le reste du jour voyez encore Alceste.

Alcide:
La voir encore?.., eh bien, differons mon départ.
Je te l'avois bien dit, je partiray trop tard.
Je vais la voir aimer un Espoux qui l'adore,
Je verray dans leurs yeux un tendre empressement:
Que je vais payer cherement
Le plaisir de la voir encore!

SCENE SECONDE.
Alcide, Straton et Lychas ensemble:
L'amour a bien des maux, mais le plus grand de tous
C'est le tourment d'estre jaloux.

SCENE TROUSIÈME.
Straton, Lychas:

Straton:
Lychas, j'ay deux mots à te dire.

Lychas:
Que veux-tu? parle; je t'entends.

Straton:
Nous sommes amis de tout temps;
Céphise, tu le sçais, me tient sous son Empire.
Tu suis par-tout ses pas: qu'est-ce que tu pretens?

Lychas:
Je pretens rire.

Straton:
Pourquoy veux-tu troubler deux Coeurs qui sont
contents?

Lychas:
Je pretens rire.
Tu veux à ton gré t'enflamer;
Chacun à sa façon d'aimer;
Qui voudra soûpirer, soûpire,
Je pretens rire.

Alcides:
Ah, Lychas! What a night! Such a sorrowful night!

Lychas:
Stay the rest of the day to see Alceste again.

Alcides:
To see her again?... ah well, let us delay my departure.
I warned you I will have left too late.
I will see her love a husband whom she adores.
I will see tenderness expressed in their eyes.
For this I will pay dearly,
for the pleasure of seeing her again!

SCENE 2
Alcides, Straton, Lychas together:
Love has its pains, but the greatest of all
is the torment of being jealous.

SCENE 3
Straton, Lychas

Straton:
Lychas, I have two words to say to you.

Lychas:
What do you want? I am listening.

Straton:
We have been friends for a long time.
Cephise, as you know, holds me under her power.
You follow her every movement; what do you intend?

Lychas:
I intend to laugh.

Straton:
Why do you want to trouble two contented hearts?

Lychas:
I intend to laugh.
Flare up as you wish;
to each his own way of loving.
He who wants to sigh, sighs,
I intend to laugh.

Straton:
J'aime et je suis aimé: laisse en paix nos amours.

Lychas:
Rien ne doit t'allarmer s'il est bien vray qu'on t'aime;
Un Rival rebutté donne un plaisir extresme.

Straton:
Un Rival quel qu'il soit importune toûjours.

Lychas:
Je voy ton amour sans colere,
Tu devrois en user ainsi:
Puisque Céphise t'a sçeu plaire,
Pourquoy ne veux-tu pas qu'elle me plaise aussi?

Straton:
A quoy sert-il d'aimer ce qu'il faut que l'on quitte?
Tu ne peux demeurer long-temps dans cette Cour.

Lychas:
Moins on a de momens à donner à l'Amour
Et plus il faut qu'on en profite.

Straton:
J'aime depuis deux ans avec fidelité:
Je puis croire, sans vanité,
Que tu ne dois pas estre un Rival qui m'alarme.

Lychas:
J'ai pour moy la nouveauté,
En amour c'est un grand charme.

Straton:
Céphise m'a promis un coeur tendre, et constant.

Lychas:
Céphise m'en promet autant.

Straton:
Ah sue te croyois! ... Mais tu nés pas croyable.

Lychas:
Croy-moy, fais ton profit d'un reste d'amitié,
Sers-toy d'un avis charitable
Que je te donne par pitié.

Straton:
I love and am loved: leave our love in peace.

Lychas:
Nothing should alarm you if you are truly loved.
A rebuffed rival only bestows extreme pleasure.

Straton:
Any rival whatever is always an intruder.

Lychas:
I see your love without feeling.
You should exploit it this way:
Since Cephise knows how to please you,
why should she not please me, too?

Straton:
What is the use of loving someone whom one must
leave?
You cannot stay for long at this court.

Lychas:
The fewer moments one devotes to love
the more one must make of them.

Straton:
I have loved her faithfully for two years.
I can believe, without vanity;
there should not be a rival who alarms me.

Lychas:
I have novelty on my side.
In love, that is a great charm.

Straton:
Cephise promised me a tender and constant heart.

Lychas:
Cephise promised me the same.

Straton:
Ah, if I believed you ... but it is incredible.

Lychas:
Believe me, take the remnants of a friendship,
heed friendly advice,
which I offer you out of pity.

Straton:
Le mespris d'un coeur volage
Doit estre un assez grand mal,
Et c'est un nouvel outrage
Que la pitié d'un Rival.
Elle vient, l'infidelle,
Pour chanter dans les leux dont je prens soins icy.

Lychas:
Je te laisse avec elle,
Il ne tiendra qu'à toy d'estre mieux éclaircy.

SCENE QUATRIÈME.
Céphise, Straton:

Céphise:
Dans ce beau jour, quelle humeur sombre
Fais-tu voir à contre-temps?

Straton:
C'est que je ne suis pas du nombre
Des Amants qui sont contents.

Céphise:
Un ton grondeur et severe
N'est pas un grand agrément;
Le chagrin n'avance guere
Les affaires d'un Amant.

Straton:
Lychas vient de me faire entendre
Que je n'ay plus ton coeur, qu'il doit seul y pretendre,
Et que tu ne vois plus mon amour qu'à regret?

Céphise:
Lychas est peu discret...

Straton:
Ah je m'en doutois bien qu'il vouloit me surprendre.

Céphise:
Lychas est peu discret
D'avoir dit mon secret.

Straton:
Comment! il est donc vray! tu n'en fais point d'excuse?
Tu me trahis ainsi sans en estre confuse?

Straton:
The scorn of a fickle friend
is a great offence,
and it is a new outrage
to receive the pity of a rival.
She is coming, the unfaithful one,
to sing in the festivities in which I take part.

Lychas:
I shall leave you alone with her.
It is up to you to be better enlightened.

SCENE 4
Cephise, Straton

Cephise:
Oh this fair day, what somber humor
do I see?

Straton:
It is because I am not among
the lovers who are content.

Cephise:
A grumbling and severe tone
is not very pleasant;
Sorrow does not advance
the cause of a lover.

Straton:
Lychas has just informed me
that your heart is no longer mine, that he alone has it,
and that you have only regret for my love.

Cephise:
Lychas is indiscreet.

Straton
Ah, I suspected he was trying to lead me astray.

Cephise:
Lychas is indiscreet
to have disclosed my secret.

Straton:
What! Then it is true! You do not even seek an excuse?
You thus betray me without shame?

Céphise:
Tu te plains sans raison;
Est-ce une trahison
Quand on te desabuse?

Straton:
Que je suis estonné de voir ton changement!

Céphise:
Si je change d'Amant
Qu'y trouves-tu d'étrange?
Est-ce un sujet d'estonnement
De voir une Fille qui change?

Straton:
Apres deux ans passez, dans un si doux lien,
Devois-tu jamais prendre une chaine nouvelle.

Céphise:
Ne contes-tu pour rien
D'estre deux ans fidelle?

Straton:
Par un espoir doux, et trompeur,
Pourquoy m'engageois-tu dans un amour si tendre?
Faloit-il me donner ton coeur
Puis que tu voulois le reprendre?

Céphise:
Quand je t'offrois mon coeur, c'estoit de bonne foy
Que n'empesche-tu qu'on te l'oste?
Est-ce ma faute
Si Lychas me plaist plus que toy?

Straton:
Ingrate, est-ce le prix de ma perseverance?

Céphise:
Essaye un peu de l'inconstance:
C'est toy qui le premier m'apris à m'engager,
Pour recompense
Je te veux aprendre à changer.

Straton et Céphise:
Il faut aimer/changer toûjours.
Les plus douces amours
Sont les amours fidelles/nouvelles.

Cephise:
You have no reason to complain.
Is it betrayal
when one is disabused?

Straton:
I am astonished to see your change!

Cephise:
If I change lovers
why do you find it strange?
Is it astonishing
to see a girl who changes?

Straton:
After two years of such a blissful tie,
you should never take a new relationship.

Cephise:
Do they count for nothing,
these two faithful years?

Straton:
By sweet and misleading hope,
why have given me such a tender love?
When you gave me your heart
did you intend to take it back?

Cephise:
When I offered you my heart it was in good faith.
Why do you blame me if I take it back?
Is it my fault
if Lychas pleases me more than you?

Straton:
Ungrateful one, is this the reward for my perseverance?

Cephise:
Try a bit of inconstancy:
It was you who first taught me to commit myself.
In exchange
I shall teach you how to change.

Straton and Cephise:
One must always love/change.
The sweetest loves
are faithful/new love.

SCENE CINQUIÈME.
Licomède, Straton, Céphise:

Licomède:
Straton, donne ordre qu'on s'apreste
Pour commencer la Feste.

Straton se retire, et Licomède parle à Céphise:

Enfin, grace au dépit, je gouste la douceur
De sentir le repos de retour dans mon coeur.
J'estois à preferer au Roy de Thessalie;
Et si pour sa gloire on publie
Qu'Apollon autrefois luy servit de Pasteur,
Je suis Roy de Scyros, et Thétis est ma Soeur.
J'ay sçeu me consoler d'un himen qui m'outrage,

J'en ordonne les/eux avec tranquilité.

Qu'aisément le dépit dégage
Des fers d'une ingrate Beauté!
Et qu'apres un long esclavage
Il est doux d'estre en liberté!

Céphise:
Il n'est pas seur toûjours de croire l'apparence:
Un Coeur bien pris, et bien touché,
N'est pas aisément détaché,
Ny si tost guery que l'on pense;
Et l'Amour est souvent caché
Sous une feinte indifference.

Licomède:
Quand on est sans esperance,
On est bien tost sans amour.
Mon Rival a la preference,
Ce que j'aime est en sa puissance,
Je perds tout espoir en ce jour:
Quand on est sans esperance
On est bien tost sans amour.

Voicy l'heure qu'il faut que la Feste commence.
Chacun s'avance.
Preparons-nous.

SCENE 5
Lycomedes, Straton, Cephise.

Lycomedes:
Straton, give the order that all be made ready
for the Fete to commence.

Straton withdraws and Lycomedes speaks to Cephise:

At last self-esteem has brought
Peace back to my heart.
The King of Thessaly was preferred to me;
And if in the name of his glory it is proclaimed
That Apollo was formerly his Herdsman,
I am King of Scyros and Thetis is my sister.
I consoled myself for a loss caused by a hymen that
outraged me,
Without remorse I now order the festivities to
commence.

How easily self-esteem disengages a Lover
From the irons of an ungrateful Beauty!
And after a long period of slavery
How delightful it is to be free again!

Cephise:
Impressions are not always trustworthy:
A smitten heart
is not easily detached,
nor is it as quickly healed as might be thought;
and Love is often concealed
beneath feigned indifference.

Lycomedes:
When one is without hope,
one is soon without love.
My Rival is preferred,
the object of my love is in his power,
all hope is lost for me this day:
When one is without hope,
one is soon without love.

The hour has come for the fete to commence.
All come forth;
let us make ready.

SCENE SIXIÈME.
Le choeur, Admète, Alceste,
Phérès, Alcide, Lychas, Céphise, et Straton.

Le coeur:
Vivez, vivez, heureux Espoux.

Phérès:
Jouissez des douceurs du noeud qui vous assemble.

Admète et Alceste:
Quand l'Himen et l'Amour sont bien d'accord
ensemble,
Que les noeuds qu'ils forment sont doux!

Le choeur:
Vivez, vivez, heureux Espoux.

SCENE SEPTIÈME.
Des Nymphes de la Mer, et des Tritons, viennent faire
une Feste Marine, ou se meslent des Matelots, et des
Pescheurs.

Deux Tritons:
Malgré tant d'orages,
Et tant de naufrages,
Chacun à son tour
S'embarque avec l'Amour.
Par tout où l'on meine
Les Coeurs amoureux,
Qn voit la Mer pleine
D'Escueils dangereux,
Mais sans quelque peine
Qn n'est jamais heureux:
Une ame constante
Apres la tourmente
Espere un beau jour.
Malgré tant d'orages,
Et tant de naufrages,
Chacun à son tour
S'embarque avec l'Amour.

SCENE 6
Chorus: Admetus, Alcestis, Pheres, Alcides, Lychas,
Cephise and Straton.

Chorus:
Long live the happy couple!

Pheres:
Rejoice in the gentle bonds that unite you.

Admetus and Alcestis:
When Hymen and Love agree,

how sweet are their ties!

Chorus:
Long live the happy couple!

SCENE 7
Sea Nymphs and Tritons enter to take part in a sea
fete in which mingle mariners and fishermen.

Two Tritons:
Despite so many storms,
and so many shipwrecks,
each in turn
embarks with Love.
Wherever one finds
amorous hearts,
the sea abounds in
dangerous reefs.
But without any pain
one is never happy:
A constant heart
after torment
hopes for a fine day.
Despite so many storms,
and so many shipwrecks,
each in turn
embarks with Love.

Un Coeur qui differe
D'entrer en affaire
S'expose à manquer
Le temps de s'embarquer.
Une ame commune
S'estonne d'abord,
Le soin l'importune,
Le calme l'endort,
Mais quelle fortune
Fait-on sans quelque effort?
Est-il un commerce
Exempt de traverse?
Chacun doit risquer.
Un Coeur qui differe
D'entrer en affaire,
S'expose à manquer
Le temps de s'embarquer.

Céphise vestuë en Nymphe de la Mer, chante au
milieu des Divinitez Marines qui luy respondent.

Jeunes Coeurs, laissez vous prendre,
Le peril est grand d'attendre.
Vous perdez d'heureux moments
En cherchant à vous defendre;
Si l'Amour a des tourments
C'est la faute des Amants.

Une Nymphe de la Mer chante avec Céphise.

Plus les Ames sont rebelles
Plus leurs peines sont cruelles,
Les plaisirs doux et charmants
Sont le prix des Coeurs fidelles:
Si l'Amour a des tourments
C'est la faute des Amants.

Licomède a Alceste:
On vous apreste
Dans mon Vaisseaux
Un divertissement nouveau.

Licomède et Straton:
Venez voir ce que nostre Feste
Doit avoir de plus beau.

A heart that delays
to commit itself
may not have time
to embark.
A common heart
is astonished at first.
Unwanted care
lulls it to sleep.
But what success
comes without effort?
Is there a business
without a downturn?
Everyone must take a chance.
A heart that delays
to commit itself
may not have time
to embark.

Cephise dressed as a Sea Nymph sings in the midst of
the Sea Divinities who answer her.

Young hearts, be not reticent,
it is perilous to delay.
You lose happy moments
while you seek to protect yourselves.
If love has torments
it is the fault of lovers.

A Sea Nymph sings with Cephise.

The more rebellious are the spirits
the more cruel are their sorrows.
Sweet and charming pleasures
are the reward of faithful hearts.
If love has torments,
it is the fault of lovers.

Lycomedes to Alcestis:
There is prepared
in my ship
a new entertainment.

Lycomedes and Straton:
Come see that our celebration
is the most beautiful.

*Licomède conduit Alceste dans son Vaisseau, Straton y
meine Céphise, et dans le temps qu'Admète et Alcide y
veulent passer, le Pont s'enfonce dans la Mer.*

Admète et Alcide:
Dieux! le Pont s'abisme dans l'eau.

Le Coeur des Thessaliens:
Ah quelle trahison funeste.

Alceste et Céphise:
Au secours, au secours.

Alcide:
Perfide...

Admète:
Alceste...

Alcide et Admète:
Laissons les vains discours.
Au secours, au secours.

*Les Thessaliens courent s'embarquer pour suivre
Licomède.*

Le Choeur des Thessaliens:
Au secours! au secours.

SCENE HUITIÈME.
Thetis, Admète

Thétis sortant de la Mer:
Espoux infortuné redoute ma colere,
Tu vas haster l'instant qui doit finir tes jours.
C'est Thétis que la Mer revere,
Que tu vois contire toy du party de son Frere;
Et c'est à la mort que tu cours.

Thétis:
Puis qu'on mesprise ma puissance
Que les Vents deschainez
Que les Flots mutinez
S'arment pour ma vengeance.

*Thétis rentre dans la Mer, et les Aquilons excitent une
tempeste qui agite les Vaisseaux qui s'efforcent de
poursuivre Licomède.*

*Lycomedes leads Alcestis onto his ship. Straton
escorts Cephise, and just as Admetus and Alcides are
about to embark, the bridge crumbles into the Sea.*

Admetus and Alcides:
Heavens! The gangplank is swallowed up by the waters.

Chorus of Thessalians:
Ah, such a sad betrayal.

Alcestis and Cephise:
Help, help!

Alcides:
Traitor...

Admetus:
Alcestis...

Alcides and Admetus:
Let us abandon useless talk.
Help, help.

The Thessalians run to board their vessels to pursue
Lycomedes.

Chorus of Thessalians:
Help! Help!

SCENE 8
Thetis, Admetus

Thetis, emerging from the sea:
Unfortunate Husband, fear my wrath.
You hasten the moment that will end your days.
It is Thetis, whom the sea reveres,
who sides with her brother against you;
and it is toward death you speed.

Thetis:
Since my might is scorned
may the winds be released,
may the waters rise up in mutiny
and take my revenge.

*Thetis returns into the sea and the Aquilons rage a tempest
that rocks the ships that try to pursue Lycomedes.*

SCENE NEUFIÈME.
Eole, les Aquilons, les Zephirs.

Eole:
Le Ciel protege les Heros:
Allez Admète, allez Alcide;
Le Dieu qui sur les autres preside
M'ordonne de calmer les Flots.
Allez poursuivez un Perfide.
Retirez-vous
Vents en couroux,
Rentrez dans vos prisons profondes:
Et laissez regner sur les ondes
Les Zephirs les plus doux.

L'orage cesse, les Zephirs volent et font fuir les Aquilons qui tombent dans la Mer avec les nuages qu'ils en avoient élevez, et les Vaisseaux d'Alcide et d'Admète poursuivent Licomède.

Fin du premier Acte.

SCENE 9
Aeolus, the Aquilons, the Zephyrs

Aeolus:
Heaven protects heroes.
Go forth, Admetus, go forth Alcides.
The god that presides over all the others
summons me to calm the waves.
Go forth, pursue the traitor.
Withdraw,
winds of wrath,
return to your deep prisons:
and let the gentlest Zephyrs
reign over the waters.

The tempest ceases, the Zephyrs rise and chase away the Aquilons who fall into the sea from whence they came with the clouds they had conjured up, and the ships of Alcides and Admetus pursue Lycomedes.

End of Act I

81 CARLOS PATIÑO, *Maria, Mater Dei* (ca. 1640)

from E:LPA

o clement, o compassionate, o sweet virgin, Mary.

Maria, mater Dei,
memor esto mei.
Advocata peccatorum,
audi preces famulorum.
Maria, Regina caelorum,
regna in cordibus eorum.
Maria, inclita mater,
inclina tuas aures,
almaque tuos veas
audi preces meas.
Maria, Domina beatissima,
semperque amantissima,
omniumque gratissima,
pulchra et inmaculata,
super et hera exaltata:
Audi amantem,
exaudi clamantem,
adjuva suspirantem.
Maria, clamat ad te peccator,
suspirat peccator
nunc vivens, iam moriens
in lacrimabili via.
Adjuva, fove, refove, Maria,
o clemens, o pia,
o dulcis virgo Maria.
Amen.

Mary, mother of God,
remember me.
Advocate of sinners,
hear the pleas of your servants.
Mary, queen of heaven,
reign in our hearts.
Mary, revered mother,
bend your ear,
look kindly on your servants,
hear my prayers.
Mary, most blessed lady,
always most loving,
most gracious of all women,
beautiful and immaculate,
lady exalted in heaven:
hear one who loves you,
listen to one who calls to you,
respond to one who sighs.
Mary, a sinner calls out to you,
a sinner sighs,
living now, but dying
on this road of tears.
Respond, protect, revive, Mary,
oh clement, oh compassionate,
oh sweet virgin Mary.
Amen.

82 JUAN GUTIÉRRIEZ DE PADILLA, *A siolo flasiquiyo* (1653)

from MEX:Pc

Introdución

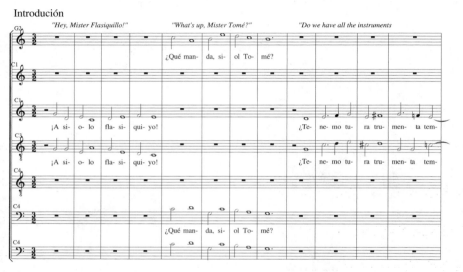

"Hey, Mister Flasiquillo!"   *"What's up, Mister Tomé?"*   *"Do we have all the instruments*

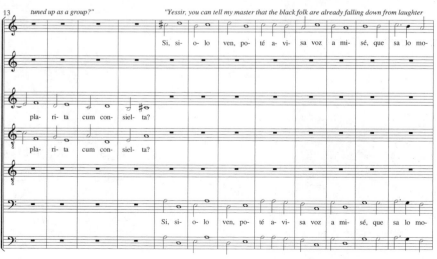

tuned up as a group?"   *"Yessir, you can tell my master that the black folk are already falling down from laughter*

and dying to dance."   *"Call him, call him quickly!*

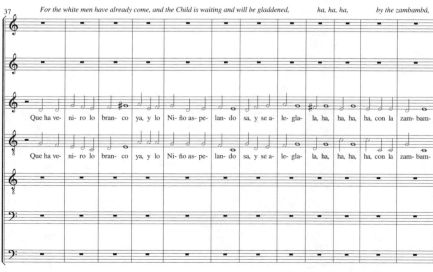

For the white men have already come, and the Child is waiting and will be gladdened,   *ha, ha, ha,*   *by the zambambá,*

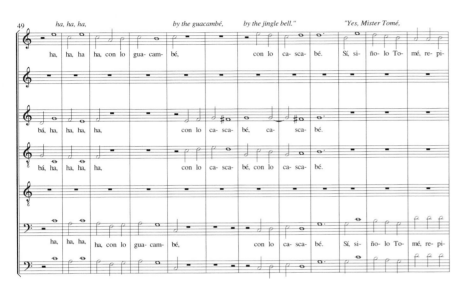

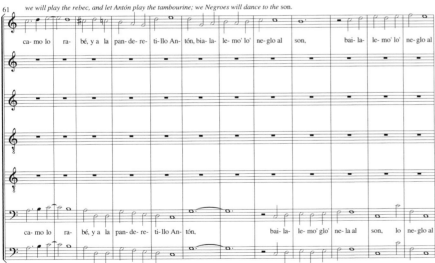

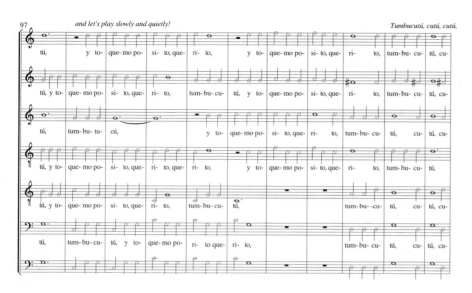

and let's play slowly and quietly!

Tumbucutú, cutá, cutá,

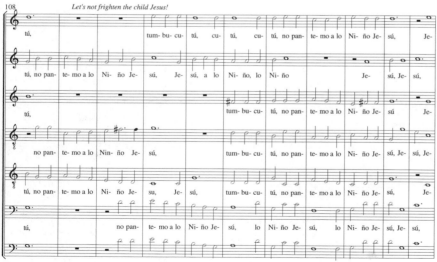

Let's not frighten the child Jesus!

GO TO THE NEXT COPLA

All of us Negroes from Guinea who are invited come:
Adé brings his servant girl; Mangla comes in his livery;

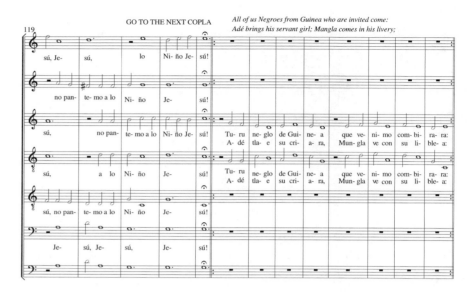

so that   the white man can see   that we serve a white King,   in jest, Adé, with a stick, pokes at and tickles

Copla 2

RETURN TO THE *RESPONSIóN*

As a doctor and surgeon, let Michael get dressed quickly,
for Jesus Christ cure our wounds with his hand.

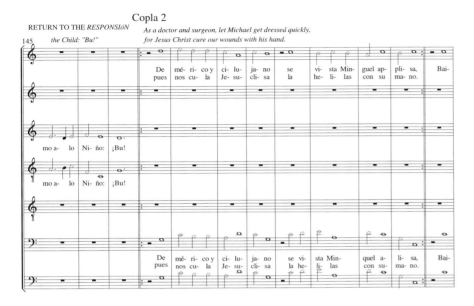

Antonilo with his sash that be brought from Puerto Rico,
will come out dressed as a monkey, and Michael as a parrot;

and when

Let's dance the canary and the villano; but one shouldn't go behind a mule that kicks or a bull that says "Moo."

I come to worship Him, I'll say to the Child, "If You weep for me, I will be happy for You."

RETURN TO THE *RESPONSIóN*
AND STOP AT THE FERMATA

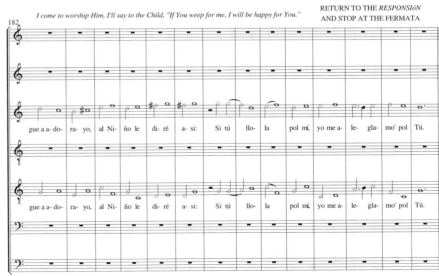

"¡Ah, siolo Flasiquillo!"
"¿Qué manda, siol Tomé?"
"¿Tenemo tura trumenta
templarita cum consielta?"
"Si, siolo ven, poté
avisa voz a misé,
que sa lo moleno ya
cayendo de pula risa
y mulliendo por baila."
"¡Llámalo, llámalo aplisa!
que ha veniro lo branco ya,
y lo Niño aspelando sa,
y se aleglala
ha ha ha ha,
con la zambambá
ha ha ha ha,
con lo guacambé,
con lo cascabé."
"Sí, siñolo Tomé,
repicamo lo rabé
y a la panderetillo Antón
bailalemo' lo' neglo al son."

¡Tumbucutú, cutú, cutú,
y toquemo posito, querito!
¡Tumbucutú!
¡No pantemo a lo Niño Jesú!

1. Turu neglo de Guinea
que venimo combirara:
Adé tlae su criara,
Mungla ve con su liblea;
y plu que lo branco vea
que Re brano nos selvimo,
con vaya Adé un lamo, plimo,
y halemo a lo Niño: "¡Bu!"

"Hey, Mister Flasiquillo!"
"What's up, Mister Tomé?"
"Do we have all the instruments
tuned up as a group?"
"Yessir, you can
tell my master
that the black folk are already
falling down from laughter
and dying to dance."
"Call him, call him quickly!
for the white men have already
come, and the Child is waiting
and will be gladdened,
ha, ha, ha,
by the zambambá,
ha, ha, ha,
by the guacambé,
by the jingle bell."
"Yes, Mister Tomé,
we will play the rebec,
and let Antón play the tambourine;
we Negroes will dance to the *son*."

Tumbucutú, cutú, cutú,
and let's play slowly and quietly!
Tumbucutú!
Let's not frighten the Child Jesus!

1. All of us Negroes from Guinea
who are invited come:
Adé brings his servant girl;
Mungla comes in his livery;
so that the white man can see
that we serve a white King,
in jest, Adé, with a stick, pokes at
and tickles the Child: "Bu!"

Tumbucutú, cutú, cutú

2. De mérico y cilujano
se vista Minguel aplisa,
pues nos cula Jesuclisa
la helilas con su mano.
Baile el canario y villano,
más no pase pol detlás
de mula que da la ¡zas!,
de toro que dirá "Mu."

Tumbucutú, cutú, cutú

3. Antonilo con su sayo,
que tlujo re Puelto Rico,
saldrá vestiro re mico,
y Minguel re papagayo;
y cuando llegue a adorayo,
al Niño le diré asi:
"Si tú llola pol mí,
yo me aleglamo' pol Tú."

Tumbucutú, cutú, cutú

Tumbucutú, cutú, cutú

2. As a doctor and surgeon
let Minguel get dressed quickly,
for Jesus Christ cures
our wounds with his hand.
Let's dance the canary and the villano;
but one shouldn't go behind
a mule that kicks
or a bull that says "Moo."

Tumbucutú, cutú, cutú

3. Antonilo with his sash
that be brought from Puerto Rico,
will come out dressed as a monkey,
and Minguel as a parrot;
and when I come to worship him,
I'll say to the Child,
"If You weep for me,
I will be happy for You."

Tumbucutú, cutú, cutú

83 JUAN BLAS DE CASTRO, *Estávase el aldeana* (ca. 1625)

from D:Mbs, Mus. Ms. E200, transposed down a fourth

from the source

Copla

[Fine]

[Return to the estrivo 𝄋]

Tañen a la queda,
mi amor no viene,
algo tiene en el campo
que le detiene.

A la queda tañen,
espadas quitan,
con su esposo cena
quien tiene dicha.

A salir del día
se fue mi ausente,
algo tiene en el campo
que le detiene.

Qué mal hizo en irse
tan da mañana,
si a la medianoche
venir pesava.

Cena, esposa y cama
non me le buelven,
algo tien en el campo
que le detiene.

Cargados los altos carros
de espigas doradas llevan,
y a sus rústicos cantares
van ayundando las ruedas.

A todos pregunta Silvia,
pero con mucha verguença
de que recién desposada,
por cuidadosa la tengan.

El zagal de Inés venía,
el de Casilda y Lorença;
como son amigos suyos
crecen su imbidia y su pena.

Quando vio que y tañían
la campana de la queda
a recojer los mancebos,
dió llorando a la puerta:

Tañen a la queda,
mi amor no viene,
algo tiene en el campo
que le detiene.

They are sounding lights-out,
my love is not coming,
there is something in the field
that detains him.

Lights-out is sounding,
the swords are put away;
the lucky one
dines with her husband.

At daybreak
my absent one left,
there is something in the field
that detains him.

What trouble is caused by leaving
so early in the morning,
if by midnight
he intended to return.

Neither dinner, wife, nor bed
bring him back to me;
there is something in the field
that detains him.

The tall carts carry
golden sheaves,
and to their rustic song
the wheels join in.

Sylvia asks everyone,
but with much shame,
if, though recently married,
they consider her watchful.

Inés's lad came,
and those of Casilda and Lorença;
since they are his friends,
her envy and pain increase.

When she saw that they are sounding
the bell for lights-out
to call in the boys,
she said, while weeping at the gate:

They are sounding lights-out,
my love is not coming,
there is something in the field
that detains him.

Estávase el [la] aldeana
a las puertas de su aldea,
viendo venir por la tarde
los zagales de las eras.

The village girl was
at the gate of her village
watching the evening return
of the lads to the farmyard.

84 FRANCISCO CORREA DE ARAUXO, *Quinto tiento de medio registro de baxones de premier tono* (1626)

from his *Libro de tientos y discursos de musica practica, y theorica de organo* (Alcala, 1626)

85 JUAN BAUTISTA JOSÉ CABANILLES, *Tiento XXIV de falses 8. punt alt* (ca. 1690)

from Spain, Felanitx (Mallorca), Biblioteca de Mn.

Cosme Bauzà

86 MANUEL RODRIGUES COELHO, *Outra Ave Maris stella* (1620)

from his *Flores de musica para o instrumento*

de tecla & harpa (Lisbon, 1620)

87 GASPAR SANZ, *Jacaras* (1675)

from his *Instrucción de música sobre la tuitarra
española . . . libro segundo* (Zaragoza, 1674)

88 WOLFGANG CARL BRIEGEL, *Was frag ich nach der Welt!* (1670)

from *Geistliche Oden Andreas Gryphii* (Gotha, 1670)

Was frag ich nach der Welt!
Sie wird in Flammen stehn.
Was acht ich reiche Pracht!
Der Tod reisst alles hin.
Was hilft die Wissenschaft,
Der mehr denn falsche Dunst?
Der Liebe Zauberwerk is tolle Phantasie.
Die Wollust ist fürwahr
Nichts als ein schneller Traum,
Die Schönheit ist wie Schnee;
dies Leben ist der Tod.

Dies alles stinkt mich an,
drum wünsch ich mir den Tod,
weil nichts, wie schön und stark,
wie reich es sei, kann stehn.
Oft, eh man leben will,
ist schon das Leben hin.
Wer Schätz' und Reichtum sucht,
was sucht er mehr als Dunst?
Wenn dem der Ehrenrauch
entsteckt die Phantasie,
so träumt ihm, wenn er wacht,
er wacht und sorgt im Traum.

Auf, meine Seel, auf, auf,
entwach aus deinem Traum!
Verwirf, was irdisch ist,
und trotze Not und Tod!
Was wird dir, wenn du wirst
vor jenem Throne stehn,
die Welt behilflich sein?
Wo denken wir doch hin?
Was blendet den Verstand?
Soll dieser leichte Dunst
bezaubern mein Gemüt
mit solcher Phantasie?

What do I care about the world!
It will go up in flames.
what heed do I pay to splendor!
Death carries everything away.
What good is knowledge,
so much more false haze?
The magic of love is a crazy fantasy.
Lust is indeed
Nothing but a fleeting dream;
beauty is like snow;
this life is death.

To me, all this stinks,
for that reason I wish death for myself,
because no matter how beautiful and great,
how rich it be, nothing can remain.
Often, before one wants to live,
life is already over.
Whoever looks for treasure and wealth,
what does he look for except haze?
If the smoke of honor
arises from the imagination,
he dreams it, if he waits,
he waits and cares in the dream.

Up, my soul, up, up;
awaken from your dream!
Reject what is earthly,
in spite of need and death!
What will happen to you, when you
stand before that throne?
Will the world assist you?
Where are we thinking of, therefore?
What blinds the mind?
Should this light haze
charm my mind
with such a fantasy?

Bisher, und weiter nicht!
Verfluchte Phantasie!
Nichtswertes Gaukelwerk,
verblendungsvoller Traum!
Du schmerzenreiche Lust!
Du folterharter Tod!
Ade, ich will nunmehr
auf freien Füßen stehn
und treten, was mich trat!
Ich eile schon dahin,
wo nichts als Wahrheit ist,
kein bald verschwindend Dunst.

Treib, ewig helles Licht,
den dicken Nebeldunst,
die blinde Lust der Welt,
die tolle Phantasie,
die flüchtige Begierd
und dieser Güter Traum
hinweg und lehre mich
recht sterben vor dem Tod!
Laß mich die Eitelkeit
der Erden recht verstehn,
entbinde mein Gemüt
und nimm die Ketten hin!

Nimm, was mich und die Welt
verkuppelt! Nimm doch hin
der Sünden schwere Last!
Laß ferner keinen Dunst
verhüllen mein Gemüt,
und alle Phantasie
der eitel-leeren Welt
sei vor mir als ein Traum,
von dem ich nun erwacht!
Und laß nach diesem Tod
wenn hin Dunst, Phantasie,
Traum, Tod, mich ewig stehn!

This much and no more!
Cursed fantasy!
Worthless illusion,
beguiling dream!
You painful pleasure!
You demanding death!
Farewell, I now choose
to stand on my own feet
and step on what stepped on me!
I already hurry to
where nothing is but the truth,
no soon-disappearing haze.

Drive out, eternally bright light,
the thick misty haze,
the blind pleasure of the world,
the crazy fantasy,
the fleeting pleasure
and these dreams of goods,
away and teach me
properly to die before death!
Let me rightly understand the vanity
of the earth,
release my mind
and remove my chains!

Take that which binds me and the world
together! Take also
the heavy load of sins!
Let furthermore no haze
wrap my mind,
and all fantasy
of the vain, empty world
be before me as a dream,
from which I now awaken!
And after this death,
when haze, fantasy,
dream, and death are gone, let me remain eternally!

89a "Joseph, lieber Joseph mein," the traditional song reconstructed

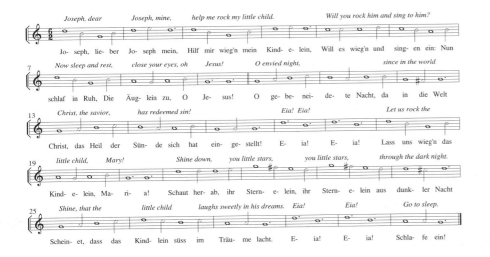

Joseph, lieber Joseph mein,
Hilf mir wieg'n mein Kindelein,
will es wieg'n und singen ein:
Nun schlaf in Ruh,
Die Äuglein zu,
O Jesus!
O gebeneidete Nacht, da in die Welt
Christ, das Heil der Sünde wich hat eingestellt!
Eia! Eia!
Lass uns wieg'n das Kindelein, Maria!
Schaut herab, ihr Sternelein aus dunkler Nacht
Scheinet, dass das Kindlein süss in Träume lacht.

Eia! Eia! Schlafe ein!

Joseph dear, Joseph mine,
help me rock my little child.
Will you rock him and sing to him?
Now sleep and rest,
close your eyes,
oh Jesus!
O envied night, since in the world
Christ, the savior, has redeemed sin!
Eia! Eia!
Let us rock the little child, Mary!
Shine down, you little stars, through the dark night.
Shine, so that the little child laughs sweetly in his dreams.

Eia! Eia! Go to sleep.

89b PHILIPP FRIEDRICH BÖDDECKER, *Natus est Jesus* (1651)

from his *Sacra partitura* (Strasbourg, 1651)

Natus est Jesus.
Natus est Deus.
Natus est Salvator noster.
Venite laeti.

Jesus is born.
God is born.
Our Savior is born.
Come happily.

Joseph, lieber Joseph mein,
bring mir der die Kindelein,
dass ich's Kindlein lege drein,
und fein sanft es schlafe ein.
Ei Joseph.

Joseph, dear Joseph mine,
bring me here the little child,
so I can lay the little child down,
and softly put him to sleep,
eh, Joseph.

Venite omnes,
portate munera,
offerte laudes,
venite dico,
venite omnes,
et cum laetitia cantate.

Come everyone,
bring gifts,
offer praise,
come, I say,
come everyone
and sing with joy.

Joseph, trag das Kindelein,
bis ich mach das Bettelein,
küss und herz das Jesulein, Eia.

Joseph, hold the little child,
while I make his little bed,
kiss and hug the little Jesus, oh.

O altitudo,
O dulcis Virgo,
O pulchra Mater,
tu peperisti splendorum nostrum.

Oh, highest one,
oh sweet virgin,
oh beautiful mother,
you bore our shining light.

Joseph gib das Kindelein,
dass ich's leg in das Krippelein,
Nun schlaf mein liebes Kindelein,
Gott der will dein Vater sein. Eia.

Joseph, give the little child to me,
so I can lay him in his little crib.
Now sleep, my dear little child,
God wants to be your father, eh.

O Jesu parvule,
Jesu dulcissime,
laude dignissime,
Rex gloriosissime,
da nos laudemus te
et cantemus in aeternum.
Alleluja.

Oh, Jesus, little child,
sweetest Jesus,
most worthy of praise,
most glorious King,
grant that we may praise you
and sing eternally.
Allelulia!

90 MATTHIAS WECKMANN, *Zion spricht: Der Herr hat mich verlassen* (1663)

from Lüneburg, Ratsbücherei, Mus. ant. prac. KN 207/6

NB: Diß Stück muß durchaus langsam und affettuos gemachet werden.

NB: This piece must be performed slowly and expressively throughout.

Zion spricht:
Der Herr hat mich verlassen,
der Herr hat mein vergessen.
Kann auch eine leibliche Mutter,
ihres Kindleins vergessen,
daß sie sich nicht erbarme
über den Sohn ihres Leibes?
Und ob sie schon desselbigen vergässe,
so will ich doch dein nicht vergessen.
Denn siehe, in meine Hände
hab ich dich gezeichnet,
spricht der Herr, dein Erlöser.

Zion says:
The Lord has abandoned me,
the Lord has forgotten me.
Can even a flesh-and-blood mother
forget her little child,
so that she does not take pity
on the son of her body?
And even if she forgot him,
I will not forget you.
For behold, on my hand
I have drawn the image of you,
says the Lord, your savior.

91 CHRISTOPH BERNHARD, *Euch ist's gegeben zu wissen das Heheimnis* (1665)

from his *Geistlicher Harmonien erster*

Theil . . . opus primum (Dresden, 1665)

Euch ist's gegeben zu wissen das Geheimnis des reichs Gottes, den andern aber in Gleichnissen, daß sie es nicht sehen, ob sie es schon sehen und nicht verstehen, oh sie es schon hören.

Unto you it is given to know the mysteries of the kingdom of God, but to others in parables, that seeing they might not see, and hearing they might not understand.

Das aber ist das Gleichnis: Der Same ist das Wort Gottes. Die aber an dem Wege sind, das sind die, die es hören, danach kömmt der Teufel und nimmt das Wort von ihrem Herzen, daß sie nicht glauben und selig werden.

Now the parable is this: The seed is the word of God. Those by the wayside are they that hear; then cometh the devil, and taketh away the word out of their hearts, lest they should believe and be saved.

Ich muß zwar am Wege der Erden hier schweben,
je dennoch laß, Jesu, dein Körnlein festkleben,
dein Körnlein des Wortes im Acker der Seele,
damit es nicht rauhe der Herrscher der Höllen.

I must hover here on the paths of the earth,
but let your seed cling, Jesus,
your seed of the word in the field of the soul,
that it may not be stolen by the ruler of hell.

Die aber auf dem Fels sind die, wenn sie es hören, nehmen sie das Wort mit Freuden an, und die haben nicht Wurzeln. Eine Zeitlang glauben sie, und zu der Zeit der Anfechtung fallen sie ab.

However, those on the rock are they who, when they hear it, receive the word with joy, and these have not root. For a while they believe, but in time of temptation fall away.

Du siehest, o Jesu, dies Herze von Steinen,
womit sich dein Same läßt schwerlich vereinen.
Erweich' es du selber, ach mach' es beständig,
damit es Anfechtung nicht mache rückwendig.

You see, oh Jesus, this heart of stone,
with which thy seed is difficult to unite.
Soften this heart, make it sure,
that temptation doth not turn it.

Das aber unter die Dornen fiel, sind die, so es hören und gehen hin unter den Sorgen, Reichtum und Wollust dieses Lebens und ersticken und bringen keine Frucht.

And that which fell among thorns are they that,
when they hear, go forth and are choked with cares
and riches and pleasures of this life, and bring no fruit
to ripeness.

Ich fühle, mein Jesu, die Dornen der Sorgen
und was sonst von Lüsten im Herzen verborgen;
die wollest du selber ausrotten, ausreißen,
damit ich befruchtet dein Garten mög' heißen.

I feel, my Jesus, the thorns of cares
and other hidden pleasures in my heart;
uproot them, tear them out,
that I may bring fruit to my garden.

Die aber auf dem guten Lande sind, sind die, die das Wort hören und behalten in einem feinen, guten Herzen und bringen Frucht in Geduld.

But those on the good ground are they who, with honest and good heart, having heard the word, keep it, and bring forth fruit with patience.

Bereite selbst, Jesu, mein Herze zum Lande,
daß es sich wohl schicke zum himmlischen Pfande,
zum Pfande des Wortes dasselbe so höre,
damit es fruchtbringend dir diene, dich ehre.

Prepare my heart, Jesus, as good soil,
that it may be fitting as a heavenly pledge,
as the pledge of the word itself,
that it may bring forth fruit in thy honor.

92a MARTIN LUTHER, "Ein feste Burg ist unser Gott" (1525)

Ein feste Burg ist unser Gott,
ein gute Wehr und Waffen;
er hilft uns frei aus aller Noth,
die uns jetzt hat betroffen.
Dear altböse Feind
mit Ernst ers jetzt meint,
groß Macht und viel List
sein grausam Rüstung ist,
auf Erd is nicht seines Gleichen.

A mighty fortress is our God,
a good shield and weapon.
He helps us freely out of all trouble
that now besets us.
The old, evil foe,
now plots in earnest;
great power and cunning
are his grim armaments.
On earth is not his like.

92b FRANZ TUNDER, *Ein feste Burg ist unser Gott* (ca. 1650)

from S:Uu, Ms. fol. 78, "Libro 2 di Motetti e Concerti

G. D. 1665," and Vok. mus 1 hdskr.

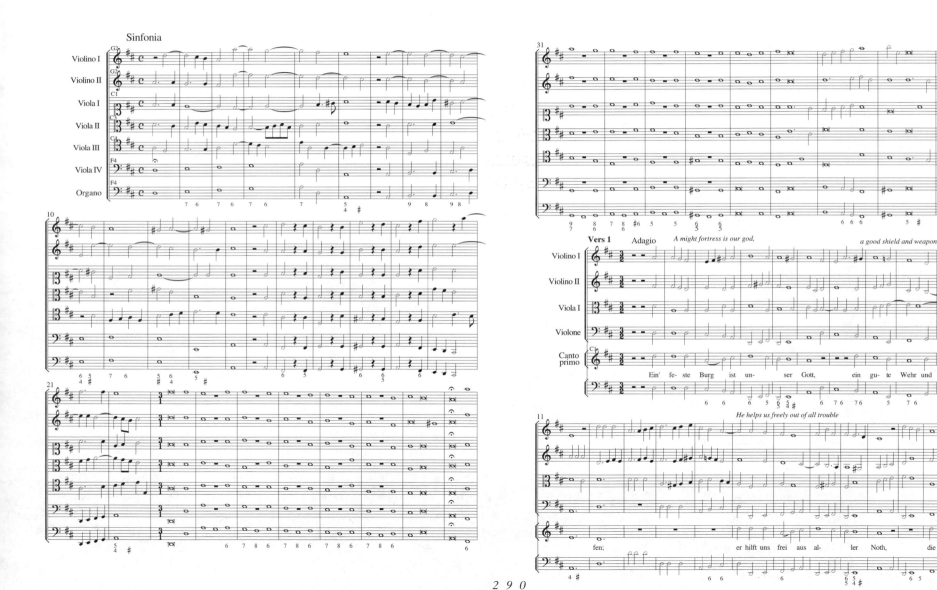

das Feld muss er be- hal- ten.

ten, das Feld muss er be- hal- ten.

ten, das Feld muss er be- hal- ten.

ten, das Feld muss er be- hal- ten.

ten, das Feld muss er be- hal- ten.

and if they wanted to overrun us completely,

Und woll- ten uns gar,

Und woll- ten uns gar,

Und woll- ten uns gar, ver- schlin-

wär und woll- ten uns gar, ver- schlin-

Vers 3. *And if the world were full of devils*

Und wenn die Welt voll Teu- fel

und woll- ten uns gar, gar ver-

und woll- ten uns gar, gar ver-

gen, gar ver-

gen, und woll- ten uns gar ver-

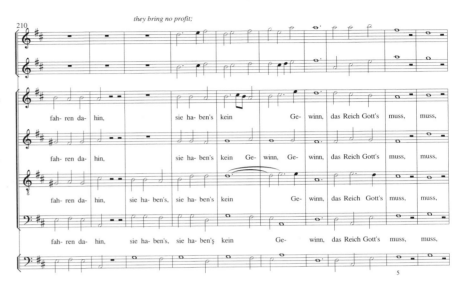

Ein feste Burg ist unser Gott,
Ein gute Wehr und Waffen;
Er hilft uns frei aus aller Noth,
Die uns jetzt hat betroffen.
Der alte böse Feind,
Mit Ernst er's jetzt meint
Groß Macht und viel List
Sein grausam Rüstung ist,
Auf Erd'n ist nicht sein's Gleichen.

Mit unsrer Macht ist nichts gethan,
Wir sind gar bald verloren.
Es streitet für uns der rechte Mann,
Den Gott selbst hat erkoren.
Fragst du, wer er ist?
Er heißt Jesus Christ,
Der Herre Zebaoth,
Und ist kein andrer Gott,
Das Feld muß er behalten.

Und wenn die Welt voll Teufel wär
Und wollten uns gar verschlingen,
So fürchten wir uns doch nicht so sehr,
Es soll uns doch gelingen.
Der Fürste dieser Welt,
Wie sau'r er sich stellt,
Thut er uns doch nicht;
Das macht, er ist gericht't,
Ein Wörtlein kann ihn fällen.

Das Wort sie sollen lassen stahn
Und keinen Dank dazu haben.
Er ist bei uns wohl auf dem Plan
Mit seinem Geist und Gaben.
Nehmen sie uns den Leib,
Gut, Ehr, Kind und Weib,
Laß fahren dahin,
Sie haben's kein' Gewinn;
Das Reich Gott's muß uns bleiben.

A mighty fortress is our God,
a good shield and weapon.
He helps us freely out of all trouble
that now besets us.
The old, evil foe,
now plots in earnest;
great power and cunning
are his grim armaments.
On earth is not his like.

With our power nothing is done.
We are very quickly lost.
The righteous man fights for us,
whom God himself has chosen.
Do you ask who he is?
He is Jesus Christ,
the Lord of Hosts,
and there is no other God;
He must hold the field.

And if the world were full of devils
and if they wanted to overrun us completely,
then we would not be at all afraid,
we must prevail.
The prince of this world.
however grim he appear,
can do nothing to us.
His power is held in check.
The least word can bring his downfall.

They shall cling to the Word,
and then receive no thanks.
Surely He is with us on the field
with His spirit and gifts.
If they take our body,
our goods, honor, children, wives,
let them all go;
they bring no profit;
the kingdom of God must remain for us.

93a Chorale "Komm, heiliger Geist, Herre Gott"

Komm, Heiliger Geist, Herre Gott,
Erfull mit deiner Gnaden Gut
Deiner Glauben Herz, Mut, und Sinn,
Dein brunstig Lieb enzund in ihn.
O Herr, durch deinen Lichtes Glast
Zu dem Glauben versammelt hast
Das Volk aus aller Welt Zungen
Das sei dir, Herr, zu Lob gesungen.
Halleluja.

Come, Holy Spirit, Lord God,
fill with your good grace
your believers' heart, courage, and mind.
Your fervent love abounds in them.
Oh Lord, by the brightness of your light,
you have joined to the believers
people from all the world and all tongues,
that praise be sung to you, Lord.
Hallelujah!

93b FRANZ TUNDER, *Komm, heiliger Geist* (ca. 1650) from Lüneburg,

Ratsbücherei der Stadt Lüneburg, Musikabteilung,

Mus. ant. pract. K.N. 209, Nr. 72

94 DIETERICH BUXTEHUDE, Passacaglia, BuxWV 161 (ca. 1680)
from D:LEm, Sammlung Becker, III.8.4

95 DIETERICH BUXTEHUDE, Praeludium, BuxWV 137 (ca. 1680)

from D:LEm, Sammlung Becker, III.8.4

Ciacona

Presto

96a Chorale "An Wasserflüssen Babylon" (Psalm 137)

An Wasserflüssen Babylon,
da saßen wir mit Schmerzen,
als wir gedachten an Zion,
da weinten wir von Herzen.
Wir hingen auf mit schwerem Mut
die Harfen und die Orgeln gut
an ihre Bäum der Weiden,
die drinnen sind in ihrem Land:
da mußten wir viel Schmach und Schand
täglich von ihnen leiden.

By the rivers of Babylon
we sat with sorrow;
as we remembered Zion
we wept from our hearts.
We hung up with sad souls
the good harps and organs
upon the branches of the willow,
which were found in their land:
then we, filled with humiliation and disrespect,
daily had to lament.

96b JOHANN PACHELBEL, *An Wasserflüssen Babylon* (ca. 1680)

from Königsberg/Ostpr., Universitätsbibliothek, Ms.

15839, and D:Bsb, Mus. ms. 30245

3

97 JOHANN HEINRICH SCHMELZER, *Corrente per l'Intrada di S.M.C.*
& di tutti i Cavaglieri

from *La contesa dell'aria e dell'acqua* (1667), published in

Arie per il balletto a cavallo [supplement to:] *Siegs-Strett und*

Der Lufft und dess Wassers Freuden-Fest und Ballet zu

Pferd . . . (Vienna, 1667)

98 JOHANN HEINRICH SCHMELZER, *Sonata Natalitia â 3 Chori Auth* (1673)

from CZ:KR

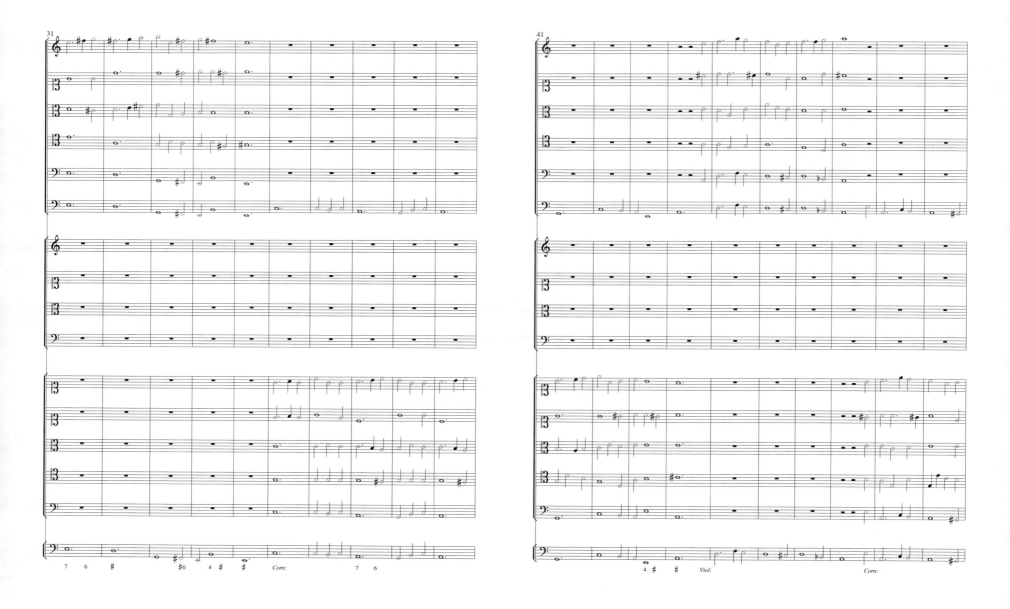

99 JOHANN ROSENMÜLLER, Sonata seconda (1667)

from his *Sonate da camera cioè sinfonie, alemande, correnti,*
balletti, sarabande, da suonare con cinque stromenti da arco,
et altri (Venice, 1667)

100 HEINRICH IGNAZ FRANZ VON BIBER, *Battalia* (1673)

from CZ-KR, B XIV 122 (A 840)

Das liederliche Schwärmen der Musquetirer, Mars, die Schlacht, Undt Lamento der Verwundten,   mit Arien imitirt Und Baccho dedicirt.
Imitating the slovenly troops of the musketeers, Mars, the battle, and lament of the wounded, with arias and dedicated to Bacchus.

Sonata

NB.: wo die Strich sindt ♪♪♪♪♪ mus man anstad des Geigens mit dem Bogen klopfen auf die Geigen, es mus wol probirt werden, der Mars ist schon bekant, aber ich hab ihn nicht bösser wissen zu verwenden, wo die Druml geth im Bass muss man an die Saite ein Papier machen dass es einen strepitum gibt, im Mars aber nur allein.

NB: Where there are marks ♪♪♪♪♪ one must hit the fiddle with the bow. It must be practiced well. Marz is already well known, but I did not know how to make him more evil. Where the drum is imitated in the bass, one must put paper on the string in order to create a snare, but only in Marz.

Die liederliche Gesellschaft von allerley Humor
The slovenly association of all kinds of humors

hic dissonant ubique, nam enim sic diversis cantilenis clamore solent
Here there are dissonances everywhere, for indeed diverse melodies are clashing.

Die Schlacht

NB: Die Schlacht muss nit mit dem Bogen gestrichen werden,
sondern mit der rechten Handt die Saite geschnelt wie die stuck, Undt starck!

*NB. The battle must not be struck with the bow,
but rather the string must be snapped with the right hand as if with a pick, and hard!*

Lamento der Verwundten Musquetirer
Lament of the wounded musketeers

101 MAURIZIO CAZZATI, Sonata settima, *La Rossella* (1656)

from his *Suonate a due violini col suo basso continuo*

per l'organo, e un altro à beneplacito per tiorba, ò violone,

Op. 18 (Bologna, 1656)

102 GIOVANNI BATTISTA VITALI, Balletto ottava and Corrente ottava (1683)

from his *Balletti, correnti, e capricci per camera,*

Op. 8 (Modena, 1683)

103 GIOVANNI MARIA BONONCINI, *Sonata XI, del secondo tuono una quarta più alto* (1672), from his *Sonate da chiesa a due violini*, Op. 6 (Venice, 1672)

104 ARCANGELO CORELLI, Sonata IV, Op. 4, no. 4 (1694)

from his *Sonate a tre . . . opera quarta* (Rome, 1694)

Giga

105 ARCANGELO CORELLI, Concerto I (ca. 1680?)

from his *Concerti grossi con duoi violini, e violoncello di
concertino obligati, a duoi altri violini, viola e basso di concerto
grosso ad arbitrio che si potranno radoppiare, Opera sesta*
(Rome, 1712)

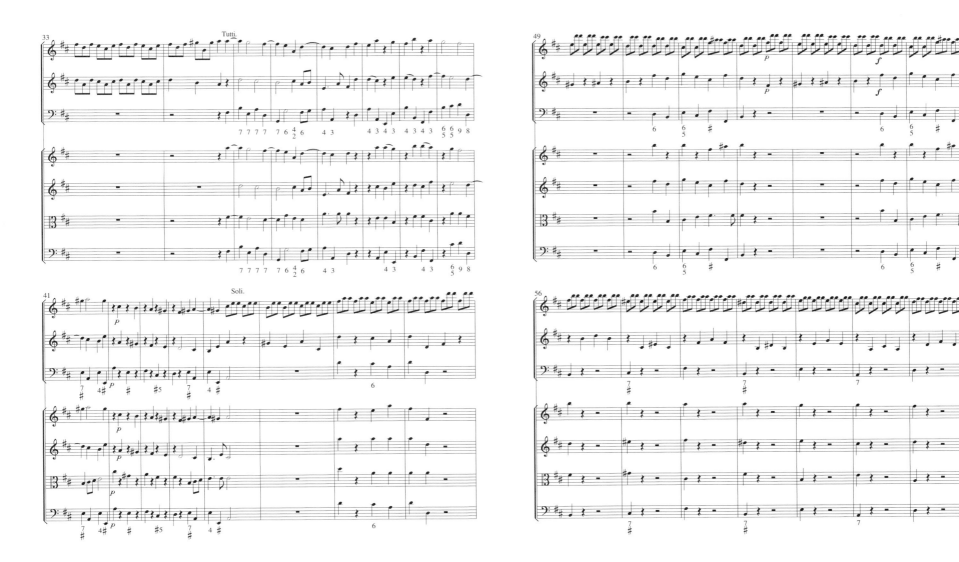

106 GIUSEPPE TORELLI, *Sinfonia con tromba e violini unissoni*, G 9 (1693?)

from I:Bsp, Lib I. 2 #4

107 ANTONIO VIVALDI, Concerto III, RV 310, Op. 3, no. 3 (1711)

from his *L'estro armonico* (Amsterdam, 1711)

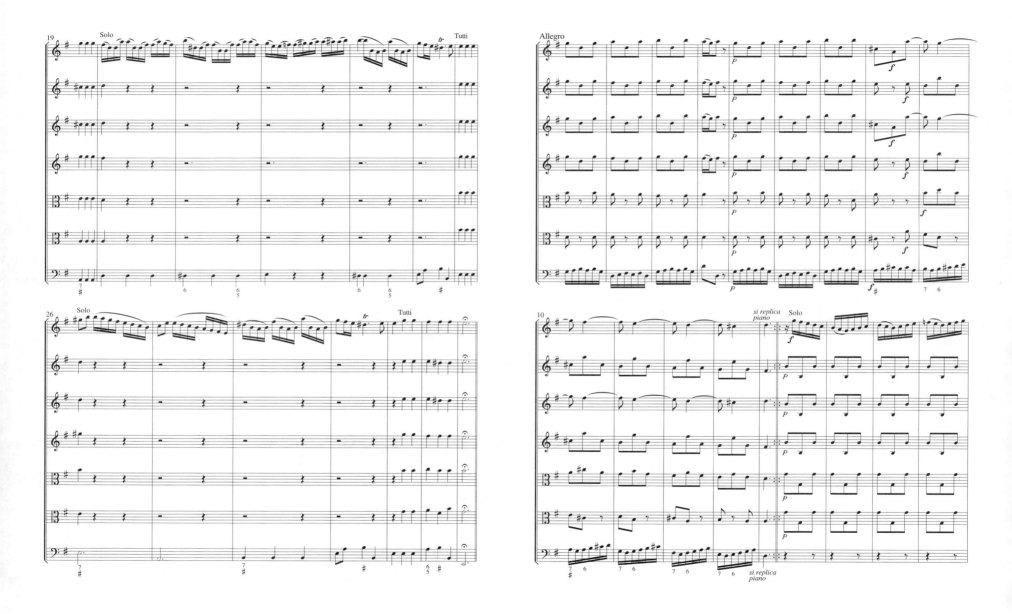

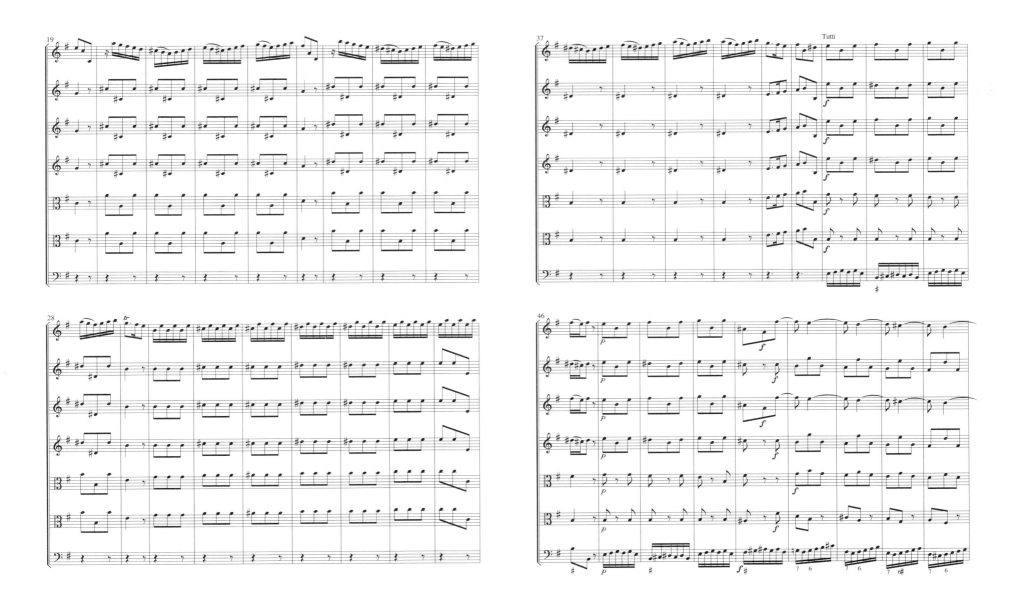

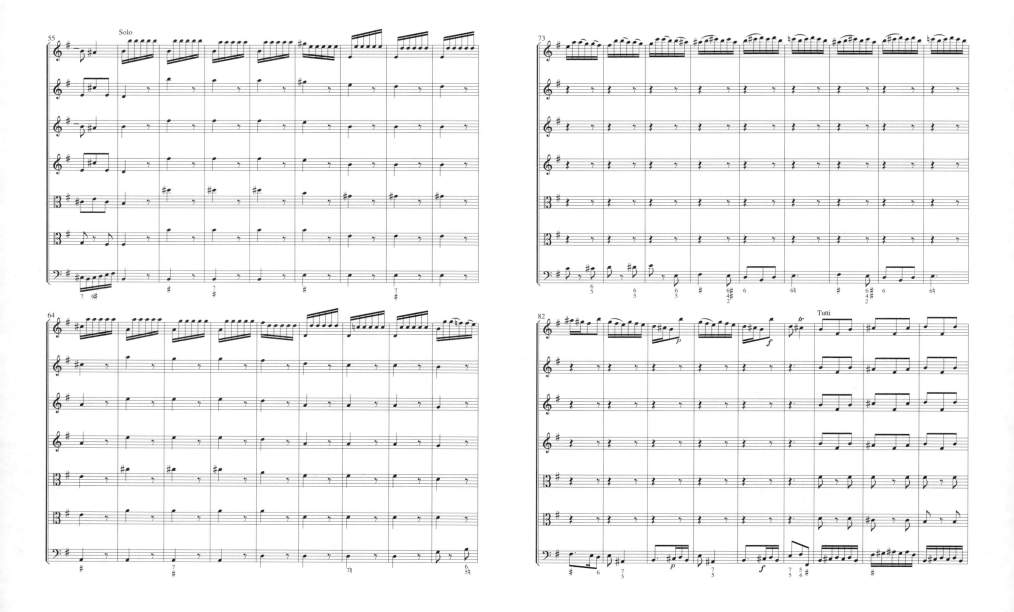

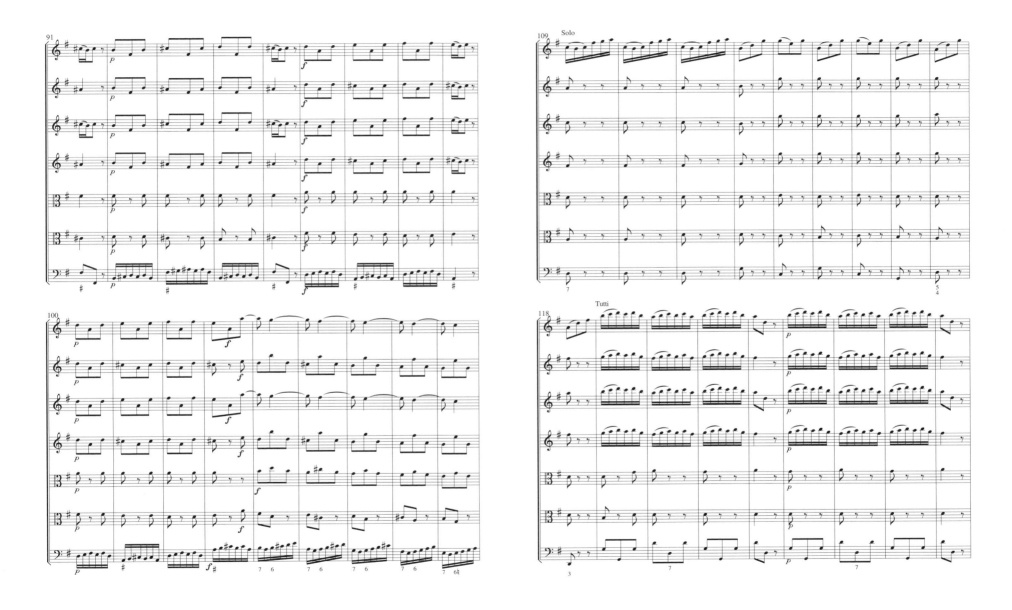

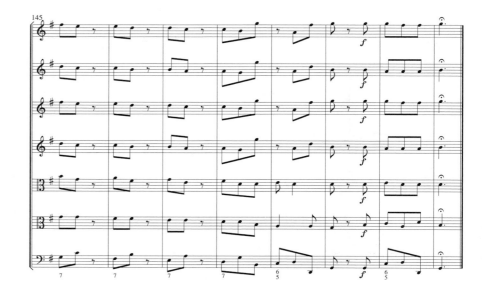

108 PELHAM HUMFREY, *Hear O Heav'ns* (ca. 1670)

from GB:Cfm, Ms. 117

Hear O heav'ns and give ear, Oh earth,
for the Lord hath spoken,
I have nourish'd and brought up children
and they have rebell'd against me.
Ah sinful nation, a seed of evildoers,
children that are corrupters,
they have forsaken the Lord.
Ah sinful nation,
they have provoked the Holy One of Israel unto anger,
Ah sinful nation.
Wash you,
make you clean,
put away the evil of your doings from before mine eyes;
cease to do evil,
learn to do well,
seek judgment,
relieve th'oppressed,
judge the fatherless,
plead for the widows.
Come now, let us reason together, saith the Lord:
Though your sins be as scarlet,
they shall be as white as snow;
though they be red like crimson,
they shall be as wool.

109 MATTHEW LOCKE, *O Be Joyful in the Lord, All Ye Lands* (1664)

from GB:Ob, MS Mus Sch c. 40

O be joyful in the Lord, all ye lands,
serve the Lord with gladness
and come before his presence with a song.
Be sure that the Lord he is God,
it is he that hath made us,
and not we ourselves;
we are his people and the sheep of his pasture.
O go your ways into his gates with thanksgiving,
and into his courts with praise;
be thankful unto him, and speak good of his name.
For the Lord is gracious,
his mercy is everlasting,
and his truth endureth from generation to generation.
Glory be to the Father,
and to the Son,
and to the Holy Ghost;
as it was in the beginning, is now, and ever shall be,
world without end. Amen.

110 MATTHEW LOCKE, "The Delights of the Bottle," from *Psyche* (1675)

from *Choice Songs and Ayres for One Voyce to Sing to
a Theorbo-Lute, or Bass-Viol, Being Most of the Newest
songs Sung at Court, and at the Publick Theatres,*
Vol. I, 2nd ed. (London, 1675)

The Delights of the Bottle, and the Charms of good Wine,
To the Pow'r and the Pleasures of Love must resign;
Though the Night in the Joys of good Drinking be past,
The Debauches but 'till the next morning doth last:
But Love's great Debauch is more lasting and strong,
for that often lasts a Man all his Life long.

Love and Wine are the Bonds that fasten us all,
The world, but for these, to Confusion would fall:
Were it not for the Pleasure of Love and good Wine,
Mankind for each trifle their Lives would resign.
They'd not value dull Life, nor would live without thinking,
Nor would Kings Rule the World, but for Love and good Drinking.

111 JOHN BLOW, *Lovely Salina* (1683)

from *Choice Ayres and Songs*, Vol. IV (London, 1683)

Lovely Salina, innocent and free
from all the dangerous Arts of Love,
thus in a melancholy Grove
enjoy'd the sweetness of her Privacy;
'till envious Gods designing to undo her,
dispatch'd the Swain not unlike then to woo her.
It was not long ere the design did take;
a gentle Youth born to persuade,
deceiv'd the too too easie Maid;
her Scrip and Garlands soon she did forsake,
and rashly told the Secrets of her Heart,
which this fond Man would evermore impart.
False Florimel, joy of my Heart, said she,
'Tis hard to love, and love in vain,
to love, and not be lov'd again;
and why should Love and Prudence disagree?
Pity ye Pow'rs that sit at ease above,
if ere you know what 'tis to be in Love.

112 HENRY PURCELL, *In Guilty Night*, Z 134 (ca. 1690)

from GB:Ob, Tenbury ms. 1175

Chorus:
In guilty night, and hid in false disguise,
forsaken Saul, to Endor comes and cries:

Saul:
Woman, arise, call pow'rful arts together,
And raise the ghost, whom I shall name, up hither.

Witch:
Why should'st thou wish me die?
Forbear, my son.
Dost though not know what cruel Saul has done?
How he has kill'd and murder'd all
that were wise and could on spirits call?

Saul:
Woman, be bold, do but the thing I wish.
No harm from Saul shall come to thee for this.

Witch:
Whom shall I raise or call? I'll make him hear.

Saul:
Old Samuel, let only him appear!

Witch:
Alas!

Saul:
What dost thou fear?

Witch:
Nought else but thee,
for thou art Saul and hast beguiled me.

Saul:
Peace, and go on, what seest thou? Let me know.

Witch:
I see the gods ascending from below.

Saul:
Who's he that comes?

Witch:
An old man mantled o'er.

Saul:
Oh! that is he, let me that ghost adore.

Samuel:
Why hast thou robb'd me of my rest to see
that which I hate, this wicked world and thee?

Saul:
Oh! I'm sore distress'd, vexed sore;
God has left me! and answers me no more;
Distress'd with war, with inward terrors too,
For pity's sake tell me, what shall I do?

Samuel:
Art thou forlorn of God and com'st to me?
What can I tell thee then but misery?
Thy kingdom's gone into thy neighbour's race,
Thine host shall fall by sword before thy face.
What can I tell thee then but misery?
Tomorrow then, till then farewell, and breathe:
Thou and thy son tomorrow shall be with me
beneath.

Chorus:
Oh! farewell.

113 JOHN BANISTER, *the Musick att the Bath* (1663)
from GB:Och, Mus. 1183

[Hornpipe]

[Saraband]

[Jig]

CHORUS

THIS CHORUS AGAIN FOR A DANCE OF FAIRIES

softly, softly steal from hence, softly, softly, softly softly steal from hence, No noise,

softly, softly steal from hence, softly, softly, softly steal, softly steal from hence, No noise,

Softly, softly steal, softly, softly, softly, softly, softly softly steal from hence, No noise,

Softly, softly steal from hence, softly, softly, softly steal from hence, No noise,

no noise dis- turb her sleep- ing sense; No noise, no noise dis- turb her sleep- ing sense.

no noise dis- turb her sleep- ing sense; No noise, no noise dis- turb her sleep- ing sense.

no noise dis- turb her sleep- ing sense; No noise, no noise dis- turb her sleep- ing sense.

no noise dis- turb her sleep- ing sense; No noise, no noise dis- turb her sleep- ing sense.

Dance for the Followers of the Night

Four in two

1st Violin

2nd Violin

Viola

Bass

Second Act Tune
Air

Alto solo:
Come all ye songsters of the sky,
Wake and assemble in this wood;
But no ill-boding bird be nigh,
No, none but the harmless, and the good.

May the God of Wit inspire,
The Sacred Nine to bear a part;
And the blessed heav'nly quire,
Shew the utmost of the art.
While Echo shall in sounds remote,
Repeat each note.

Chorus:
Now join your warbling voices all.

Soprano solo and chorus:
Sing while we trip it upon the green;
But no ill vapours rise or fall,
No nothing offend our Fairy Queen.

Night:
See, even Night herself is here,
To favour your design,
And all her peaceful train is near,
That men to sleep incline.
Let Noise and Care, Doubt and Despair,
Envy and Spite (the fiend's delight)
Be ever banish'd hence,
Let soft Repose
Her eyelids close,
And murm'ring streams
Bring pleasing dreams;
Let nothing stay to give offence.

Mystery:
I am come to lock all fast,
Love without me cannot last.
Love, like counsels of the wise,
Must be hid from vulgar eyes.
"Tis holy and we must conceal it;
They profane it, who reveal it.

Secresy:
One charming night gives more delight,
Than a hundred lucky days.
Night and I improve the taste,
Make the pleasure longer last.
A thousand sev'ral ways.

Sleep and Chorus:
Hush, no more, be silent all,
Sweet Repose has clos'ed her eyes,
Soft as feather'd snow does fall.
Softly steal from hence
No noise disturb her sleeping sense.

115 HENRY PURCELL, *Dido and Aeneas* (1689), excerpts

from GB:T, MS1266

115a ACT I

ACT I

Belinda:

Shake the cloud from off your brow,
Fate your wishes does allow;
Empire growing,
Peasures flowing,
Fortune smiles and so should you.
Shake the cloud from off your brow.

Chorus:

Banish sorrow, banish care,
Grief should ne'er approach the fair.

Dido:

Ah! Belinda, I am press'd
With torment not to be confess'd.
Peace and I are strangers grown.
I languish till my grief is known,
Yet would not have it guess'd.
Peace and I are strangers grown.

Belinda:

Grief increases by concealing.

Dido:

Mine admits of no revealing.

Belinda:

Then let me speak; the Trojan guest
Into your tender thoughts has press'd.

[Second Woman:]

The greatest blessing Fate can give,
Our Carthage to secure, and Troy revive.

Chorus:

When monarchs unite, how happy their state;
They triumph at once o'er their foes and their fate.

Dido:

Whence could so much virtue spring?
What storms, what battles did he sing?
Anchises' valour mix'd with Venus' charms,
How soft in peace, and yet how fierce in arms!

Belinda:

A tale so strong and full of woe
Might melt the rocks, as well as you.

[Second Woman:]

What stubborn heart unmov'd could see
such distress, such piety?

Dido:

Mine with storms of care oppress'd
Is taught to pity the distress'd;
Mean wretches' grief can touch,
so soft, so sensible my breast,
But ah! I fear I pity his too much.

Belinda, Second Woman, and Chorus:

Fear no danger to ensue,
The hero loves as well as you.
Ever gentle, ever smiling,
And the cares of life beguiling,
Fear no danger to ensue,
The hero loves as well as you.
Cupids strew your paths with flowers
Gather'd from Elysian bowers.
Fear no danger to ensue,
The hero loves as well as you.

115b

ACT III [scene 2]

ACT III, [SCENE 2]

Dido:
Thy hand, Belinda; darkness shades me,
On thy bosom let me rest;
More I would, but Death invades me;
Death is now a welcome guest.

When I am laid in earth, may my wrongs create
No trouble in thy breast,
Remember me! but ah! forget my fate

Chorus:
With drooping wings ye Cupids come,
And scatter roses on her tomb,
Soft and gentle as her heart;
Keep here your watch, and never part.

116 GEORGE FRIDERIC HANDEL, *Tamerlano* (1724), HWV 18, excerpts

from GB:Lbl, R.M.20.d.2

116a "Forte, e lieto a morte andrei," Act 1, scene 1

Bajazet:
Forte e lieto a morte andrei,
se celassi ai pensier miei
della figlia il grande amore.
Se non fosse il suo cordoglio,
tu vedresti in me più orgoglio,
io morrei con più valor.
Forte e lieto, ecc.

Bajazet:
Strong and happy, to death would I go
if were hidden from my thoughts
my daughter's great love.
Were it not for her sorrow,
you would see in me more pride,
I would die with more valor.
Strong and happy, etc.

116b Act I, scene 10,

Recitativo

Bajazet: *Oh happy, lucky day for me!*   *Oh dear daughter, oh Emperor, oh friends,*

Oh per me lie-to, av-ven-tu-ro-so gior-no! O fi-glia ca-ra, o Im-pe-ra-tor, o a-mi-ci;

already in my heart I am as tranquil as in expression.   *And do you know why, my daughter?*   *And do you know why, tyrant?*

già son nel cor, qual son tran-quil-lo in vol-to. E sai per-ché, mia fi-glia? E'l sai, ti-ran? da'

I am free of your bonds. Tamerlano: *But who here can save you from my fury?* Bajazet: *Who can?*   *I can.*

lac-ci tuoi son sciol-to. Ma chi di man può trar-ti al fu-ror mi-o? Chi lo può? Lo pos-s'i-o.

Violino I

Violino II

Viola

Bajazet

You tremble.   *You threaten.*   *I laugh at your fury,*   *at your threats.*

Fre-mi, mi-nac-cia; mi ri-do del tuo fu-ror, di tue mi-

Bassi
(Violoncello,
Contrabasso,
Cembalo)

Violino I, II

Bajazet   *I have defeated your pride with my poison.*

Bassi

nac-cie:. Ho vin-to l'or-go-glio tuo con mio ve-len; né

You cannot kill me,   *nor can you cause me not to die.*

puoi far-mi mo-ri-re, né far sì, ch'io non mo-ra;

This death is   *my chosen triumph,*   *at the same time your downfall*

è que-sta mor-te, il mio tri-on-fo e-let-to, già di-ven-ta tuo scor-no,

and my revenge.   Asteria: *Ah! Father,*   *what are you saying?*

e mia ven-det-ta. Ah! ge-ni-tor, che par-li?

(Va mancando nel ritirarsi dentro la scena, sostenuto sempre da Asteria ed Andronico.)
(He collapses as he goes off stage, supported all the while by Asteria and Andronico.)

Bajazet:
Oh per me lieto, avventuroso giorno!
O figlia cara, o Imperator, o amici;
Già son nel cor, qual son tranquillo in volto.
E sai perché, mia figlia?
E'l sai, tiran? da lacci tuoi son sciolto.

Tamerlano:
Ma chi di man può trarti al furor mio?

Bajazet:
Chi lo può? Lo poss'io.
Fremi, minaccia; mi rido
Del tuo furor, di tue minaccie. Ho vinto
L'orgoglio tuo, col mio velen; nè puoi
Farmi morire, nè far si, ch'io non mora:
È questa morte il mio trionfo eletto,
Già diventa tuo scorno, e mia vendetta.

Asteria:
Ah Genitor! che parli?

Bajazet:
Sì, figlia, io moro: addio.
Tu resti, ahimè, che dir non posso: in pace
Tu resti, figlia, negli affanni: e questo
È il solo affanno mio.

Asteria:
No: vo' seguirti anch'io;
Io vo' morir. Prence: Tiranno: un ferro!
Al tuo amor, al tuo sdegno, il chiedo. Ah Padre!
Con questa man, che per l'estrema volta
Ora il bacio, e co' miei pianti inondo,
Prendi un ferro, se puoi: passami il seno,
E guida teco la tua figlia.

Bjazet:
Oh sempre avversi Dei!
Dov'è ferro, o veleno?
Sì, figlia: in questi estremi amplessi miei
Per pietà del tuo duol l'ucciderei.

Bajazet:
Oh happy, lucky day for me!
Oh dear daughter, oh Emperor, oh friends,
already in my heart I am as tranquil as in expression.
And do you know why, my daughter?
And do you know why, tyrant? I am free of your bonds.

Tamerlano:
But who here can save you from my fury?

Bajazet:
Who? I can.
You tremble, you threaten, I laugh
at your fury, at your threats. I have defeated
your pride with my poison. You cannot
kill me, nor can you cause me not to die.
This death is my chosen triumph,
at the same time your downfall and my revenge.

Aseria:
Ah father! what are you saying?

Bajazet:
Yes, daughter, I am dying: farewell.
You remain, alas, I cannot say it; in peace,
you remain, daughter, in distress; and this
is my only distress.

Asteria:
No, I want to follow you.
I want to die. Prince, Tyrant, a sword!
Of your love, of anger, I ask it. Ah Father!
With this hand, as for the last time
I kiss you, and with my streaming tears,
take a sword, if you can, and stab my breast,
and take your daughter with you.

Bajazet:
Oh eternally contrary gods!
Where is a sword or poison?
Yes, daughter, in these last of my embraces,
out of pity for your sorrow, I would kill you.

Figlia mia, non pianger, no.
Lascia allora uscire il pianto,
quando morto, io nol vedrò.
    Figlia, &c.

Bajazet à Temerlano:
Tu spietato, il vedrai (misera figlia!)
Ma non ne andrai lieto gran tempo. Io vado
Le Furie a scatenar per tuo tormento;
Già miro il dì mancar: morte, ti sento.
Per tuo supplizio è quest'orror. Su, via
Furie, e ministre del gran Re dell'ira:
Io vi conosco: eccovi là: quel crudo
Percotete, sbranate, lacerate.
Sì, lanciategli al core
I serpi e el Ceraste.
Degni di voi que' colpi son. Sì; presto,
Ma non cessate ahimé, se stanche siete,
La rabbia mia prendete,
O meco lo portate
Laggiù nel Regno del furore eterno.
Per tormentar, per lacerar quel mostro
Io sarò la maggior furia d'Avverno.

(Va mandando nel ritirarsi dento la scena sostenuto sempre da Asteria ed Andronico.)

My daughter, do not weep, no.
Let your tears escape
only when, dead, I will not see them.
    My daughter, etc.

Bajazet to Tamerlano:
You ruthless man, you will see it (poor daughter!)
but you will not remain happy for long. I go
to unleash the furies for your great torment.
Already I am fainting. I feel death.
This horror is your torture. Up, away,
furies and minions of the great King of Wrath.
I know you. There you are. Against that cruel man
now strike. Dismember him. Lacerate him.
Yes, strike at his heart,
serpents and monsters.
Worthy of you are those sins. Yes. Quickly,
do not stop. Alas, if you are tired,
take my wrath,
or with me take it
down into the Kingdom of Eternal Fury.
To torment, to lacerate that monster
I will be the greatest fury of hell.

(He collapses as he goes off stage, supported by Asteria and Andronico.)

117 ALESSANDRO SCARLATTI, *Cain, ovvero Il primo omicidio* (1707), Part II, excerpt

from the autograph in US:SFsc.

407

412

Abel:
Hor se braman posar la fronda, e il rio,
Trà la fronda, e il ruscel riposo anch'io.

Cain:
Più non sò trattener l'impeto interno;
Dormi, se dormir brami un sonno eterno.

Abel:
Soccorso oh Dio!

Cain:
Dio n'è lontano.

Abel:
Imploro la tua pietà.

Cain:
Replico il colpo.

Abel:
Io moro.

(Sinfonia, ch'imita colpi, poi concitata con
Instromenti da flato, ch'imitino il Tuono.)

Voce di Dio:
Cain dov'è il Fratello? Abel dov'è?

Cain:
Nól sò Signor; forse del fratel mio
Il custode son io?

Voce di Dio:
Che mai facesti? Il sangue
Del tuo German sin dalla terra esclama;
Quel cadavere esangue
Maledetto ti chiama;
Hor di strage fraterna il suolo asperso
Per tè inutil, bifolco
Negherà sempre averso,
Che germe alcun più ti produca il solco,

Disperato, e solingo
Abborrito da tutti andrai ramingo.

Abel:
Now, if the branches and the river long for rest,
among the branches and stream I do, too.

Cain:
I cannot restrain my internal impulse any longer.
Sleep, if you wish to sleep in eternal slumber.

Abel:
Help, oh God!

Cain:
God is far away.

Abel:
I beg for your pity.

Cain:
I repeat the blows.

Abel:
I am dying.

(Interlude, which imitates blows, then, combined
with wind instruments, which imitate thunder.)

Voice of God:
Cain, where is your brother? Where is Abel?

Cain:
I do not know, Lord. Am I my brother's
keeper?

Voice of God:
What have you done? The blood of your brother
calls out from the soil.
That cursed bloody corpse
calls out to you.
Now the soil, soaked by the murder of a brother,
will be useless to you, farmer,
it will be always against you.
No seed will produce anything for you in your
furrows.
Desperate and alone,
abhorred by all, you will wander . . .

Come mostro spaventevole
Da tè ogn'uno fuggirà,
E qual furia abominevole
Sempre il Cieì t'abborrirà.
Come mostro ecc.

Cain:
Signor se mi dai bando,
E dal tuo aspetto, e dalla Terra in pena
Del grave error, ch'il tuo perdon non merta

Andrò per poco errando;
Ecco, ch'ogn'un mi avena,
E la mia vita ad ogni passo è incerta.

O preservami per mia pena,
O mi fulmina per pietà.
Il timor mi rende ardito,
Quindi merto esser punito
Per l'ardir, per la viltà.
    O preservami, ecc.

Voce di Dio:
Vattene, non temer; tù non morrai;
Nella tua fronte impresso
Il mio comando havrai,
Nè ad alcun fia permesso
Di farti insulto; E chi sarà l'ardito
Sette volte di più sarà punito.

Vuò il castigo, non voglio la morte,
Che la vita tua pena sarà,
Del morire le pene son corte;
Mà il rimorso un inferno si fa.
    Vuò il castigo ecc.

Cain:
O ch'io mora vivendo,
O ch'io viva morendo,
Non cangia tempre il mio destin spietato,
che non sà d'esser vivo un disperato.

Like a terrifying monster,
everyone will flee from you,
and like an abominable fury
Heaven will always abhor you.
Like a terrifying monster, etc.

Cain:
Lord, if you banish me
from your presence and from the earth, as punishment
for my grave sin, for which I do not deserve your
pardon,
I will wander for a while,
when, behold, everyone will strike out at me,
and my life will be uncertain at every step of the way.

Either preserve me in my pain,
or strike me down, for pity's sake.
Fear makes me bold,
thus, I deserve to be punished
For boldness, for sinfulness.
    Either preserve me, etc.

Voice of God:
Go and fear not. You will not die.
On your forehead you will have imprinted
my commandment.
No one will be permitted
to attack you. And whoever attempts it
will be punished sevenfold.

I want punishment, I do not want death.
Since your life will be your punishment,
with death your pains will be shortened.
But your remorse will an inferno.
    I want punishment, etc.

Cain:
Either I die by living
or live while dying;
my horrible destiny will not change,
for a fugitive does not know how to live.

Bramo insieme, e morte, e vita,
Nè sò dir ciò, che vorrei;
Colpa mia ne sei punita
Hor, ch'il Mondo, e Dio perdei?
   Bramo ecc.

I long for death and for life at the same time,
nor do I know which I desire.
My sin is being punished,
now that I will lose God and the world.
   I long for, etc.

Voce di Lucifero:
Codardo nell'ardire, e nel timore,
Disperato Cain, dov'è il tuo core?
Tù primo figlio, e caro
Del prim'huom della terra,
Tù primiero omicida,
Primo ad espor l'imagine di guerra,
Tù primo traditore, e fratricida,
E se a morir sarai secondo, il fato
Ti destina (se vuoi) primo dannato.

Voice of Lucifer:
Coward in hope and in fear,
desperate Cain, where is your heart?
You, the first and dear son
of the first man on Earth,
you the first murderer,
the first to expose the image of war,
you the first traitor and first fratricide,
and if you are the second to die, fate
destines you (if you wish) to be the first one damned.

Nel potere il Nume imita;
E col Ciel pugna da forte;
S'ei diè legge alla tua vita,
Tù commanda alla tua morte.
   Nel potere ecc.

Imitate the power of God,
and fight strongly against Heaven.
If He set the law to your life,
you command your own death.
   Imitate the power, etc.

Cain:
Oh consigli d'Inferno, onde soggiace
D'Adam la prole al memorando esiglio,
Tradiste il padre, ed hor tentate il figlio?
Senza Dio, senza pace
Ramingo andrò; ma non vuò farmi addesso
Reo d'un fratello ucciso, e di me stesso.

Cain:
Oh counsel from Hell, which subjects
Adam's descendants to a famous exile!
You betrayed the father, and now do you tempt the son?
Without god, without peace,
I will wander aimlessly. But now I do not want to make
myself guilty of killing my brother and myself.

Miei genitori addio,
Più non vi rivedrò,
Due figli hoggi piangete,
L'uno per mè perdete,
L'altro perchè peccò.
   Miei Genitori ecc.

My parents, farewell.
I will see you no more.
Today you weep for two sons:
the one lost because of me,
the other because I sinned.
   My parents, etc.

118 ALESSANDRO SCARLATTI, *Il genio di Mitilde* (1711)

from I:MOe, Campori Appendice 2402

4 1 5

416

Il genio di Mitilde
mente non v'è, che penetrar si vanti.
Si strani ell'ha pensier,
si varii i passi,
che rende stanchi e lassi
gl'arditi spiriti
a secondaria intenti.
Ah, che tant'oltre
che poggiar mai crede.
D'onde pria si parti
tornar si vede.

Tante il mar non ha procelle,
tante in ciel non sono stelle,
quante voglie ha Mitilde nel suo cor.
Mite allor che più accarezza,
tutta sdegno poi disprezza.
Dona e toglie quando vuole
e speme e amor.

Ella muove talor per vie romite solinga
i passi a respirar tra i boschi;
poi, sdegnando le selve e gl'antri foschi
a più ameni soggiorni,
volge le piante
a viver lieti i giorni;
quindi altera e vezzosa
in ricche spoglie
pompa di sua bellezza
al guardo altrui si rende.
Cortese d'ogni cor gl'ossequi prende.
Dolce canta, favella,
e scherza e ride,
ma allor che di speranza
i cuori ingombra,
toglie fugendo
di speranza ogn'ombra.

Così d'amor lo strale
fugga chi vuoi goder
tranquilla pace
che il dardo suo fatale
uccide col piacer
che alletta e piace.
    Così d'amor, ecc.

The whimsy of Mitilde:
no mind can boast of penetrating it.
She has such strange thoughts,
such odd tangents,
that they tire and exhaust
the daring spirits
who try to follow her.
Ah, how much beyond
capture!
Whence, before you leave,
you return.

The sea has not as many storms,
heaven has not as many stars
as Mitilde has desires in her heart.
Gentle at first, while she caresses,
then, all scorn, she despises.
She gives and takes away, when she wishes,
both hope and love.

She moves, at times, along solitary paths, alone,
to withdraw among the woods.
Then, leaving the forests and the dark caves
for more amusing places,
she leaves the bushes
to live happy days.
Then, proud and charming,
richly dressed,
she makes her own beauty
noticed by others.
Charmingly, she wins every heart;
she sweetly sings, speaks,
jokes, laughs.
But while she fills
hearts with hope,
she flees,
removing every shadow of hope.

Thus may he
flee Love's arrow, whoever would enjoy
tranquil peace,
since the fatal dart
kills with pleasure
that entices and pleases.
    Thus may he, etc.

119 ANTONIO VIVALDI, *Jubilate, o amoeni chori* and *Gloria in excelsis Deo*
RV 588 (1717), first three movements

from I:Tn, Foà 40.

119a Introduzione
Aria: Jubilate o amoeni Chori

119b Recitativo: In tam solemni pompa

119c Gloria

Gloria in exelsis Deo

Aria:
Jubilate, o amoeni chori,
divo amori
laetos plausus mille date.
Et in vocibus canoris
summi honoris
caeli et terra resonate.

Recitative:
In tam solemni pompa
armonice cantamus
et Deo immortali honores mille damus.
Vos mecum, o cantores,
suaviter canentes
jubilamus dicentes:

Aria and chorus:
Sonoro modulamine
voce simul unanimi
nunc proferamus jubilo:
Gloria in excelsis Deo
Nunc proferamus jubilo:
Gloria in excelsis Deo
Concentu gravi et tenero
repetant etiam citharae,
fistulae, lirae et organa.
Gloria in excelsis Deo,

Aria:
Rejoice, oh joyful choirs,
for divine love
give thanks by the thousands.
And in melodious voices
with highest honors
let heaven and earth resound.

Recitative:
In a solemn ceremony,
harmoniously we sing,
and to god the immortal, honor by thousands we give.
With me, oh singers,
sweetly singing,
let us rejoice, saying:

Aria and chorus:
With sonorous harmonies,
as with a single voice,
now let us sing rejoicing:
Glory in the highest to God.
Now let us sing rejoicing:
Glory in the highest to God.
Harmonized with low and high,
let the strings echo,
winds, lute, and organ:
Glory in the highest to God.

120 FRANCESCO ANTONIO BONPORTI, *Ite molles, Motetto per il Signore* (1701)

from his *Motetti a canto solo con violini . . . opera terza*
(Venice, 1701)

Aria:

Ite molles ite flores
ite bellae rosae purpuratae
Christum Iesum coronate
date gratos odores
ite bellae rosae purpuratae.

Recitative:

Ardet amore anima mea.
Languet cor meum dum video te,
o dulcis Iesu, languet core meum coelisti
gaudio, laetitia inenarrabili
inflammata deficio.

Aria:

Placidi Zefiri susurrate.
Aurae molles per prata
per colles mea gaudia narrate volando.

Recitative:

Iam respiro venio ad te Coelestis sponse.

Iam sum beata.
Ego dilecto meo dilectus meus mihi.

Aria:

O quam dulce, o Iesu care
mea vita tecum stare
casto corde te amare
sponse mi amor praeclare.
Alleluia.

Aria:

Go, soft flowers,
go beautiful red rose,
crown Jesus Christ,
give welcome fragrance.
Go, beautiful red rose.

Recitative:

My soul burns with love.
My heart languishes until I see you,
oh sweet Jesus, my heart languishes for heavenly
joy, for the indescribable inflamed happiness
that I lack.

Aria:

Placid zephyrs, whisper.
Soft breeze, tell of my joy while flying
through the meadows, through the hills.

Recitative:

At last I breathe, I come to you, heavenly
bridegroom.
At last I am blessed.
I am chosen by my chosen one.

Aria:

Oh how sweet, oh dear Jesus,
to spend my life with you,
to love you with a chaste heart,
my bridegroom, my beautiful love.
Hallelujah!

121 JEAN-PHILIPPE RAMEAU, *Hippolyte et Aricie* (1733), Act IV, second half

from the first printed edition of the score.

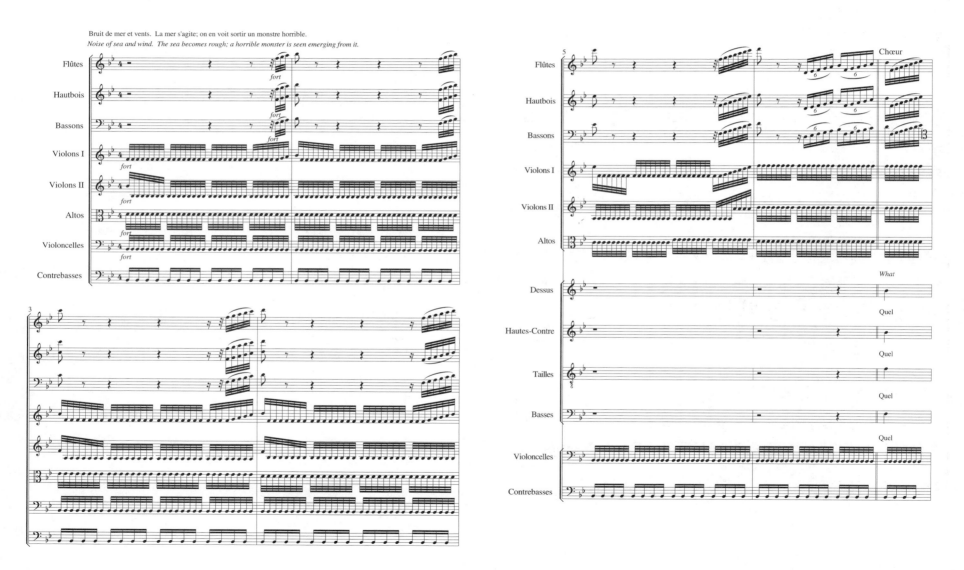

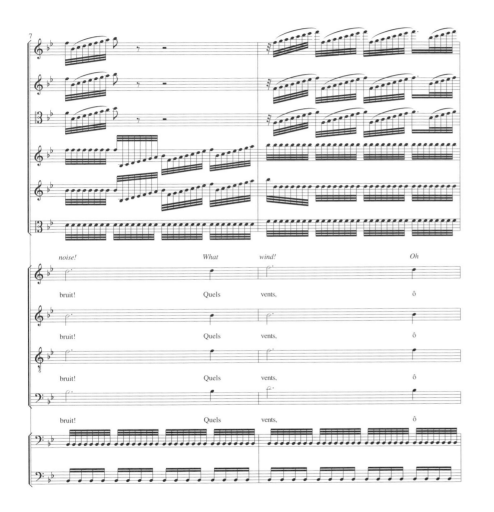

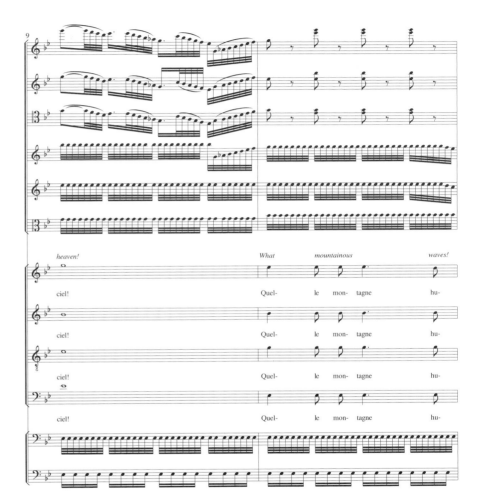

Scène IV - PHÈDRE, troupe de chasseurs et chasseresses
Scene IV - PHÈDRE, a troupe of hunters and huntresses

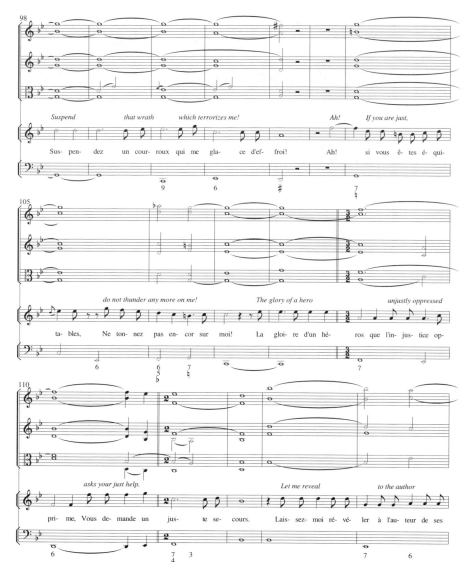

Bruit de mer et vents. La mer s'agite; on en voit sortir un monstre horrible.

Choeur:
Quel bruit! Quels vents, ô ciel! Quelle montagne humide!
Quel monstre elle enfante à nos yeux!
O Diane, accourez! Volez du haut des cieux!
Hippolyte (avançant vers le monstre):
Venez! Qu'à son défaut je vous serve de guide.

Aricie:
Arrête, Hippolyte, où cours-tu?
Que va-t-il devenir! Je frémis, je frissonne.
Est-ce ainsi que les Dieux protègent la vertu?
Diane mîme l'abandonne.

Choeur:
Dieux! Quelle flamme l'environne!

Aricie:
Quels nuages épais! Tout se dissipe . . . Hélas!
Hippolyte ne paraît pas . . .
Je meurs . . .

Choeur:
Ô disgrâce cruelle,
Hippolyte n'est plus . . .

SCÈNE 4
Phèdre, troupe de chasseurs et de chasseresses

Phèdre:
Quelle plainte en ces lieux m'appelle?

Choeur:
Hippolyte n'est plus.

Phèdre:
Il n'est plus! ô douleur mortelle!

Choeur:
Ô regrets superflus!

Phèdre:
Quel sort l'a fait tomber dans la nuit éternelle?

Noise of sea and wind. The sea becomes rough; a horrible monster is seen emerging from it.

Chorus:
What noise! What wind! Oh heaven! What mountainous waves! What a monster it brings before our eyes!
Oh Diana, run to us! Fly from the heights of heaven!
Hippolytus:
Come. In her absence I will lead you.

Aricia:
Stop, Hippolytus. Where are you going?
What will become of him? I tremble, I shudder.
Is this how the gods protect virtue?
Diana herself abandons him.

Chorus:
Gods! What a fire surrounds him!

Aricia:
What thick clouds! All has vanished . . . Alas!
Hippolytus is not to be seen . . .
I die . . .

Chorus:
Oh cruel misfortune,
Hippolytus is no more.

SCENE 4
Phaedra, a troop of hunters and huntresses

Phaedra:
What lamentation calls me to this place?

Chorus:
Hippolytus is no more.

Phaedra:
He is no more! Oh deathly sorrow!

Chorus:
Oh vain regrets!

Paedra:
What fate sent him falling into the eternal night?

447

Choeur:
Un monstre furieux, sorti du sein des flots,
Vient de nous ravir ce héros.

Phèdre:
Non, sa mort est mon seul ouvrage.
Dans les Enfers c'est par moi qu'il descend.
Neptune de Thésée a cru venger l'outrage.
J'ai versé le sang innocent.
Qu'ai-je fait? Quels remords! Ciel! J'entends le
tonnerre.
Quel bruit! Quels terribles éclats!
Fuyons! Où me cacher? Je sens trembler la terre.
Les Enfers s'ouvrent sous mes pas.
Tous les Dieux, conjurés pour me livrer la guerre,
Arment leurs redoutables bras.
Dieux cruels, vengeurs implacables!
Suspendez un courroux qui me glace d'effroi!
Ah! si vous êtes équitables,
Ne tonnez pas encor sur moi!
La gloire d'un héros que l'injustice opprime,
Vous demande un juste secours.
Laissez-moi révéler à l'auteur de ses jours
Et son innocence et mon crime!

Choeur:
Ô regrets superflus!
Hippolyte n'est plus.

Chorus:
A furious monster, from the boson of the waves,
came to rob us of this hero.

Phaedra:
No, his death is my doing, alone.
It is because of me that he has fallen into the Underworld.
Neptune believed that he avenged Theseus.
I have shed innocent blood.
What have I done? What remorse! Heavens! I hear
the thunder.
What noise! What terrible thunderclaps!
Let us flee! Where to hide myself? I feel the earth tremble.
Hell opens beneath my feet.
All the gods, sworn to make war on me,
strengthen their formidable arms.
Cruel gods, implacable avengers!
Suspend that wrath which terrorizes me!
Ah! If you are just,
do not thunder any more on me!
The glory of a hero unjustly oppressed
asks your just help.
Let me reveal to the author of his days
both his innocence and my crime!

Chorus:
Oh vain regrets!
Hippolytus is no more.

122 FRANÇOIS COUPERIN, *La Ténébreuse, Allemande* (1713)

from his *Premier livre de pièces de clavecin, troisième*

ordre (Paris, 1713)

123 FRANÇOIS COUPERIN, *Le Petit-Rien* (1722)

from his *Troisième livre de pièces de clavecin,*

quatorzième ordre (Paris, 1722)

124 ELISABETH JACQUET DE LA GUERRE, Sonata no. 2 (1707)

from her *Sonates pour le viollon et pour le clavecin*

(Paris, 1707)

125 GEORGE FRIDERIC HANDEL, *Saul*, HWV 53 (1738),

excerpts from GB: Lbl, R. M. 20.g.3

125a Act the First, scene 1. An Epincion or Song of Triumph for the
Victory over Goliath and the Philistines

Air

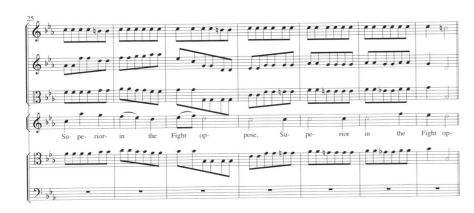

Trio Ardito

Air:
An infant rais'd by thy command,
To quell thy rebel foes,
could fierce Goliath's dreadful hand
Superior in the fight oppose.

Trio:
Along the monster atheist strode,
With more than human pride,

Chorus:
The youth inspir'd by Thee, o Lord,
With ease the boaster slew:

Chorus:
How excellent thy name, o Lord,
In all the world is known!

And armies of the living God
Exulting in his strength defied.

Our fainting courage soon restor'd,
And headlong drove that impious crew.

Above all heav'ns, o King ador'd,
How hast Thou set thy glorious throne!
Hallelujah!

125b Act the Third, scene 1. Saul disguis'd at Endor

Accompagnato

Recitative

Violino I

Violino II

Viola

Saul

Continuo

'Tis said, here lives a Wom- an, close Fa- mi- liar With th'E- ne- my of Man- kind.

He vouch- safes No An- swer to the Sons of Dis- o- be- dience!   Ev'n my own Cour- age

Her I'll con- sult, And know the Worst. Her Art is Death by Law; And while I mind- ed Law, sure Death at- tend- ed

fads' me!   Can It be?   Is Saul be- come a Cow- ard?-   I'll not be- lieve it!

Accompagnato

Such hor- rid Prac- tic- es: Yet, o hard Fate; My- self am now re- duc'd to ask the Coun- sel Of those I once ab- horr'd!

If Heav'n de- nies thee Aid,   seek it from Hell!

Scene 2, Saul and the Witch of Endor

Scene 3 Apparition of Samuel and Saul

Accompagnato
Saul:
Wretch that I am, of my own ruin author!
Where are my old supports? The valiant youth,
Whose very name was terror to my foes,
My rage has drove away. Of God forsaken,
In vain I ask his counsel! He vouchsafes
No answer to the sons of disobedience!
Even my own courage fails me! Can it be?
Is Saul become a coward? I'll not believe it!
If Heav'n denies thee aid, seek it from Hell!

Accompagnato
Saul:
'Tis said, here lives a woman, close familiar
With th'enemy of mankind: her I'll consult,
And know the worst. Her art is death by law;
And while I minded law, sure death attended
Such horrid practices. Yet, oh hard fate,
Myself am now reduc'd to ask the counsel
Of those I once abhorr'd!

SCENE 2
Saul and the Witch of Endor

Recitative
Witch:
With me what would'st thou?

Saul:
I would that by thy art thou bring me up
The man whom I shall name.

Witch:
Alas! Thou know'st
How Saul has cut off those who use this art.
Would'st thou insnare me?

Saul:
As Jehovah lives, On this account no mischief shall
befal thee.

Witch:
Whom shall I bring up to thee?

Saul:
Bring up Samuel.

Air
Witch:
Infernal spirits, by whose pow'r
Departed ghosts in living forms appear,
Add horror to the midnight hour,
And chill the boldest hearts with fear:
To this stranger's wond'ring eyes
Let the prophet Samuel rise!

SCENE 3
Apparition of Samuel and Saul

Accompagnato
Samuel:
Why hast thou forc'd me from the realms of peace
Back to this world of woe?

Saul:
O holy Prophet!
Refuse me not thy aid in this distress.
The numerous foe stands ready for the battle:
God has forsaken me: no more he answers
By prophets or by dreams: no hope remains,
Unless I learn from thee what course to take.

Samuel:
Hath God forsaken thee? And dost thou ask
My counsel? Did I not foretell thy fate,
When, madly disobedient, thou didst spare
The curst Amalekite, and on the spoil
Didst fly rapacious? Therefore God this day
Hath verified my words in thy destructions,
Hath rent the kingdom from thee, and bestowed it
On David, whom thou hatest for his virtue.
Thou and thy sons shall be with me tomorrow,
And Israel by Philistine arms shall fall.
The Lord hath said it: He will make it good.

125c Act III, scene 5

Elegy on the Death of Saul and Jonathan

Elegy on the death of Saul and Jonathan

Mourn, Israel, mourn thy beauty lost,
Thy choicest youth on Gilboa slain!
How have thy fairest hopes been crossed!
What heaps of mighty warriors strow the plain!

126 JOHANN SEBASTIAN BACH, *Passio D.N.J.C. secundum Matthaeum* ("St. Matthew Passion"), BWV 244 (1727, revised 1736), nos. 1–6

from D:Bsb, Mus. Ms. Bach P 25

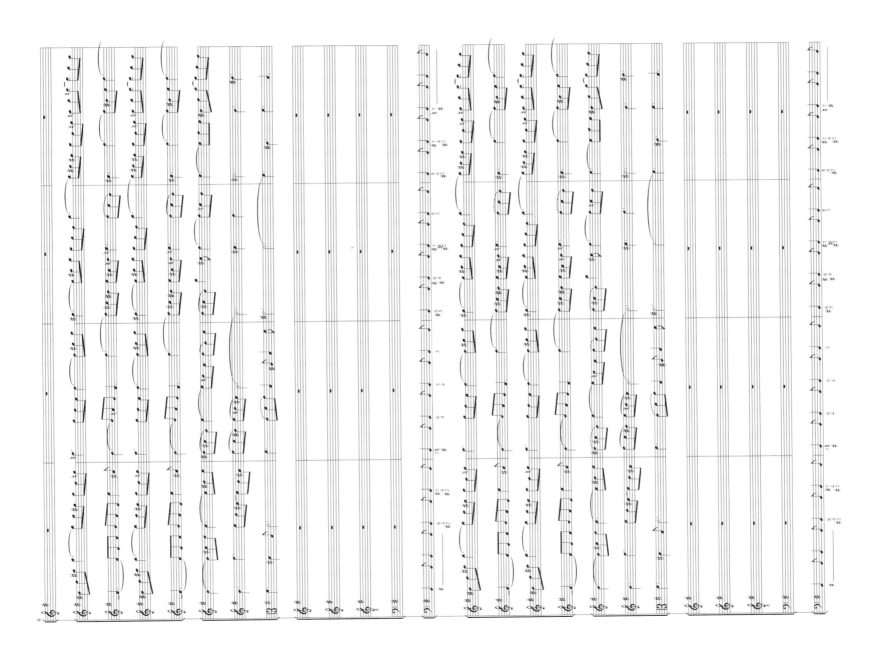

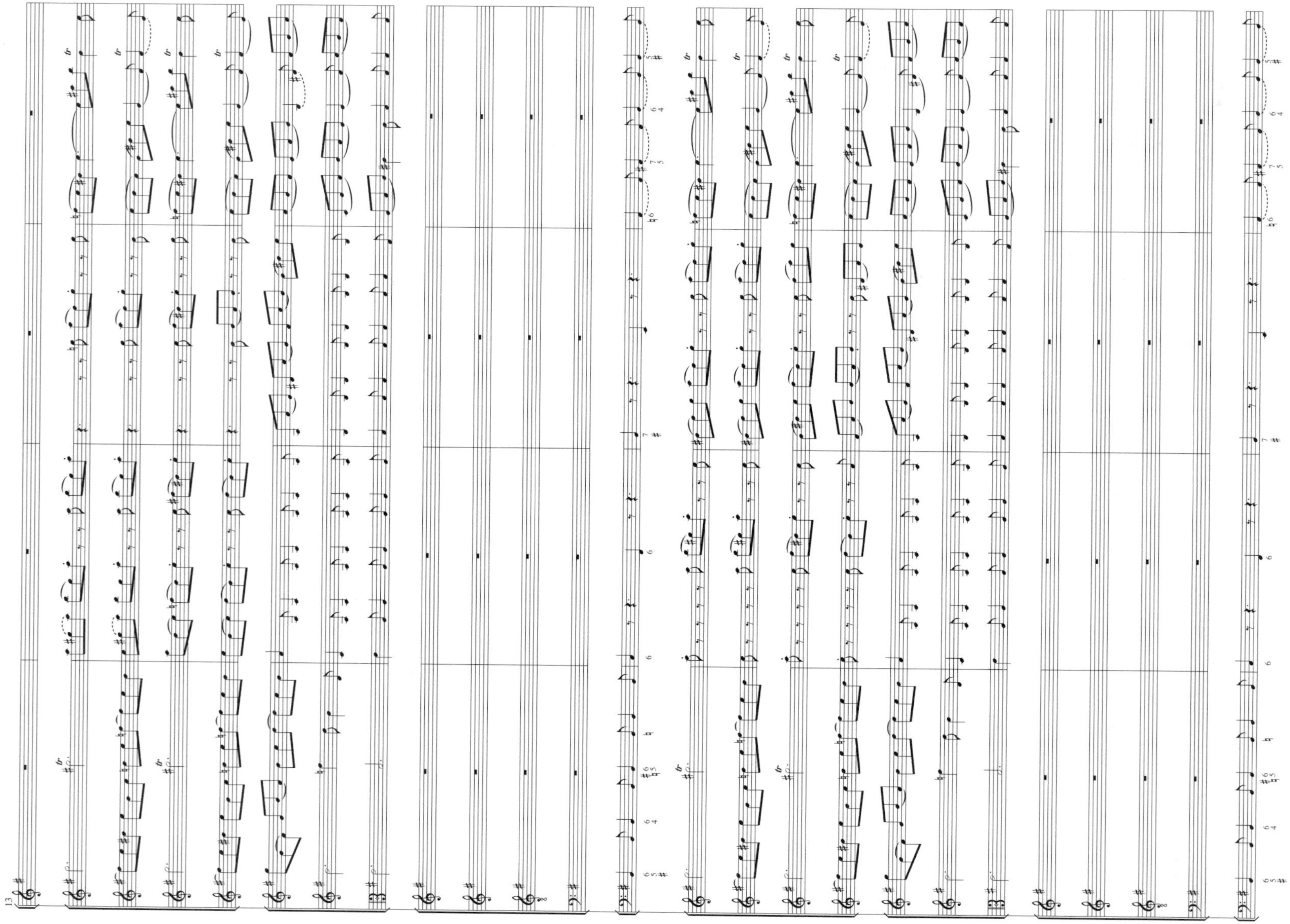

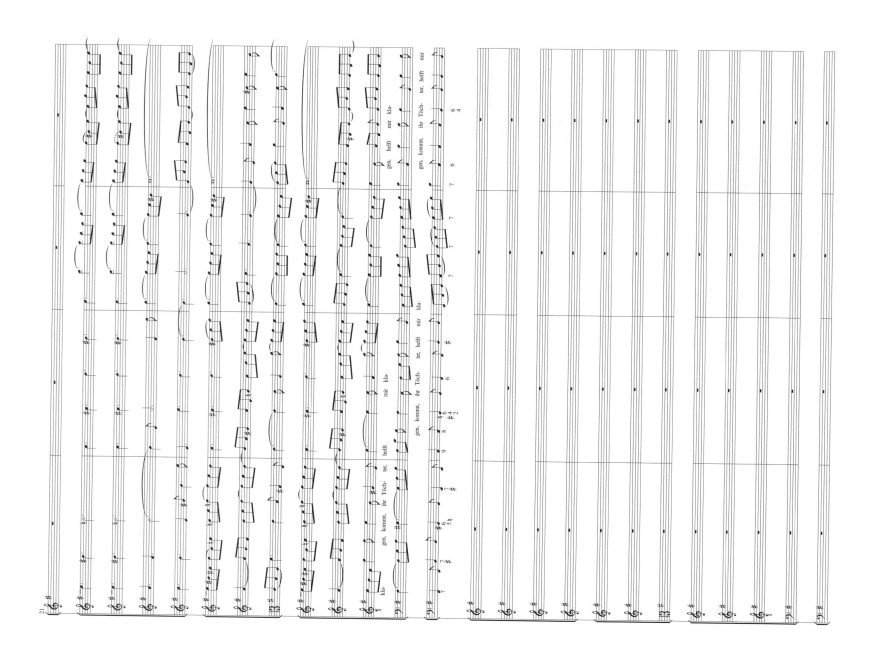

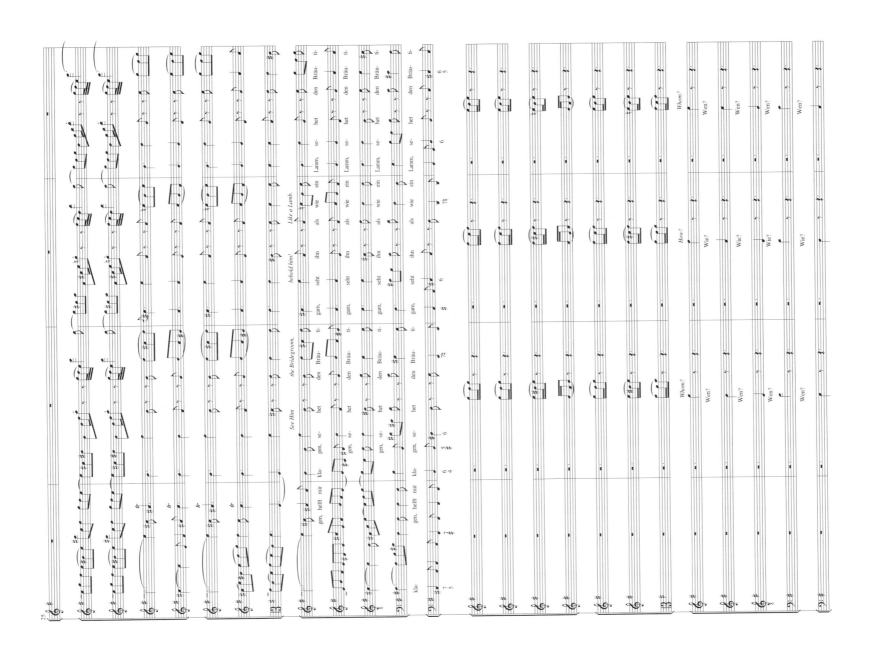

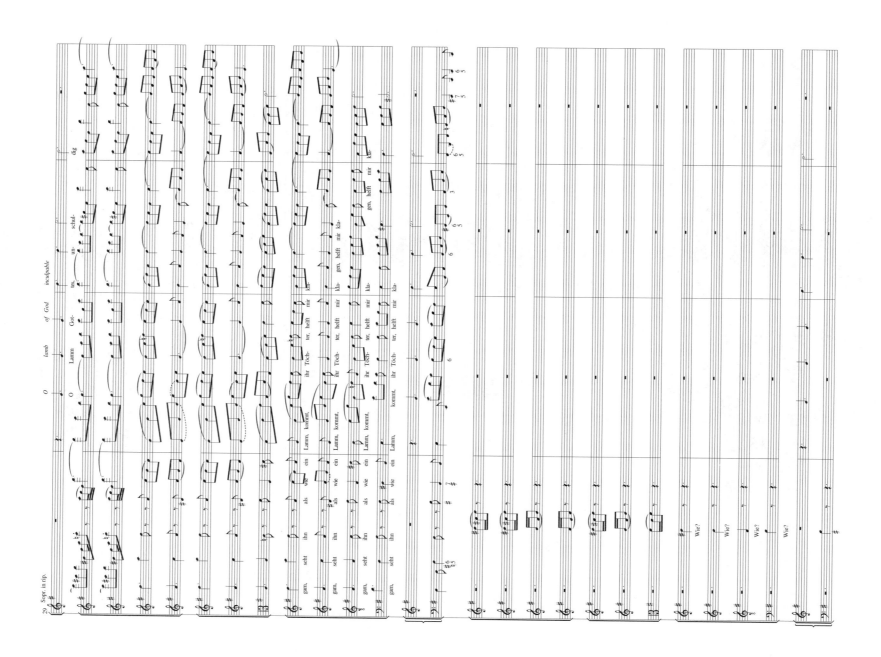

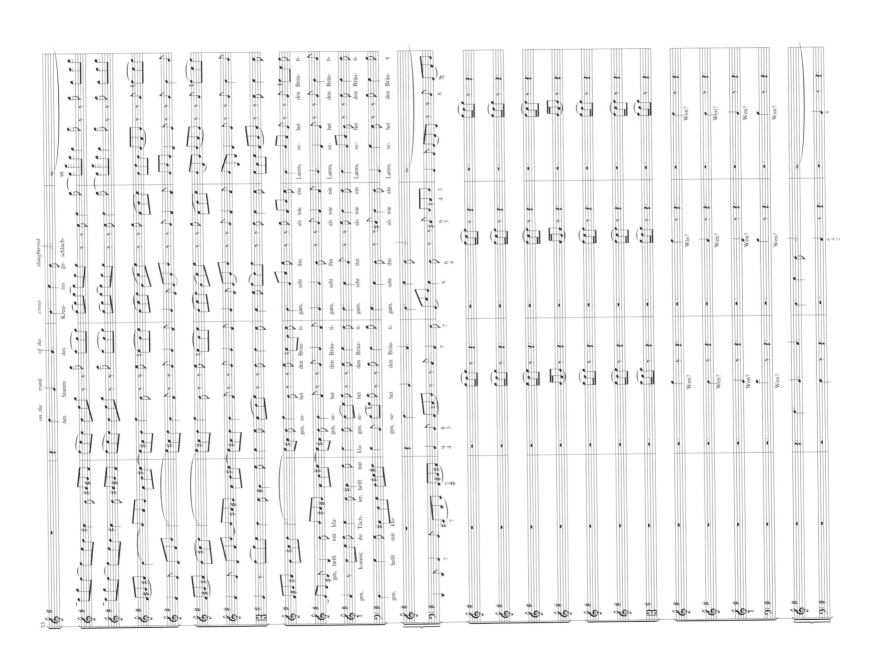

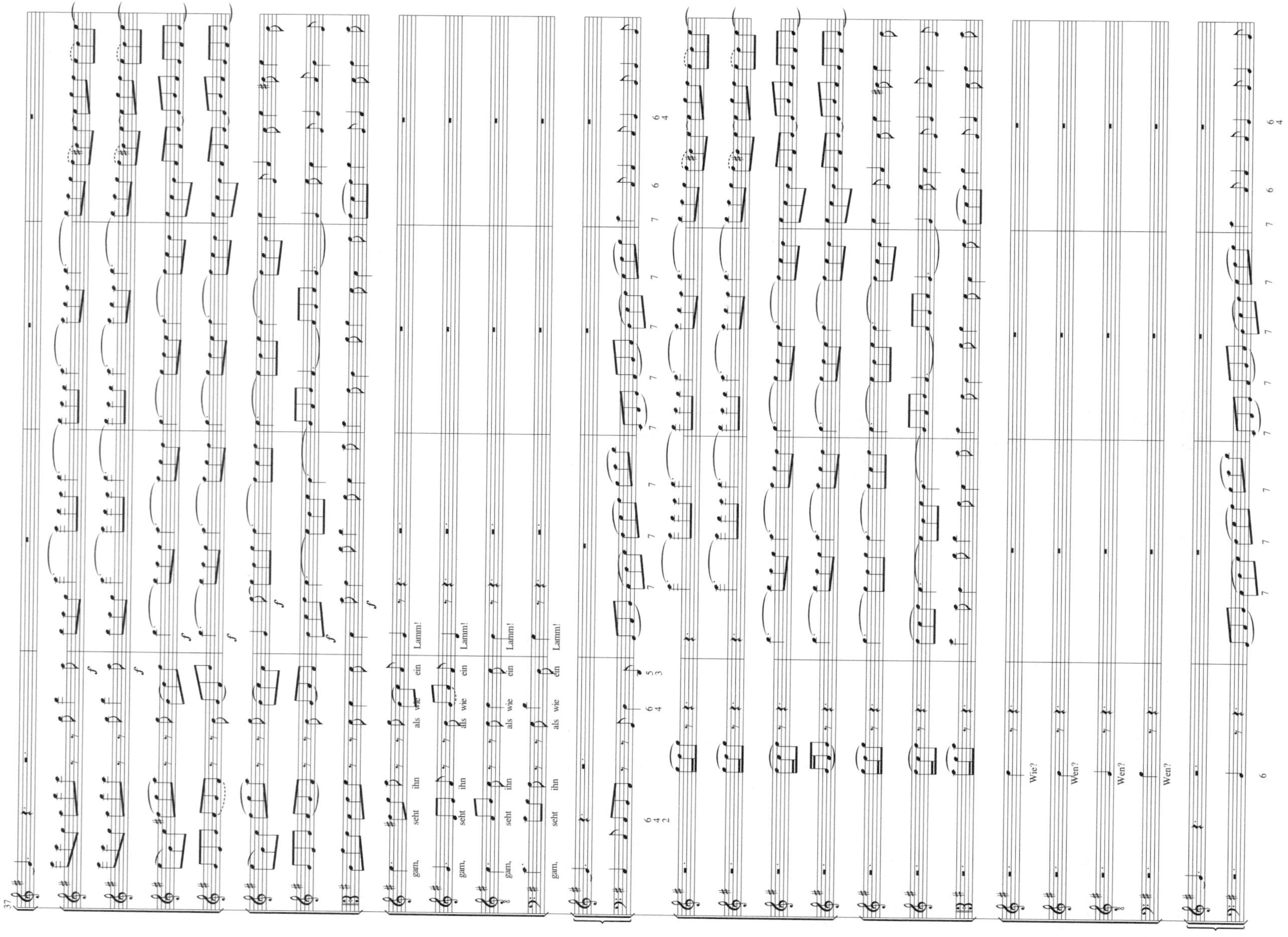
37
gam, seht ihn als wie ein Lamm!
gam, seht ihn als wie ein Lamm!
gam, seht ihn als wie ein Lamm!
gam, seht ihn als wie ein Lamm!
Wie?
Wen?
Wen?
Wen?

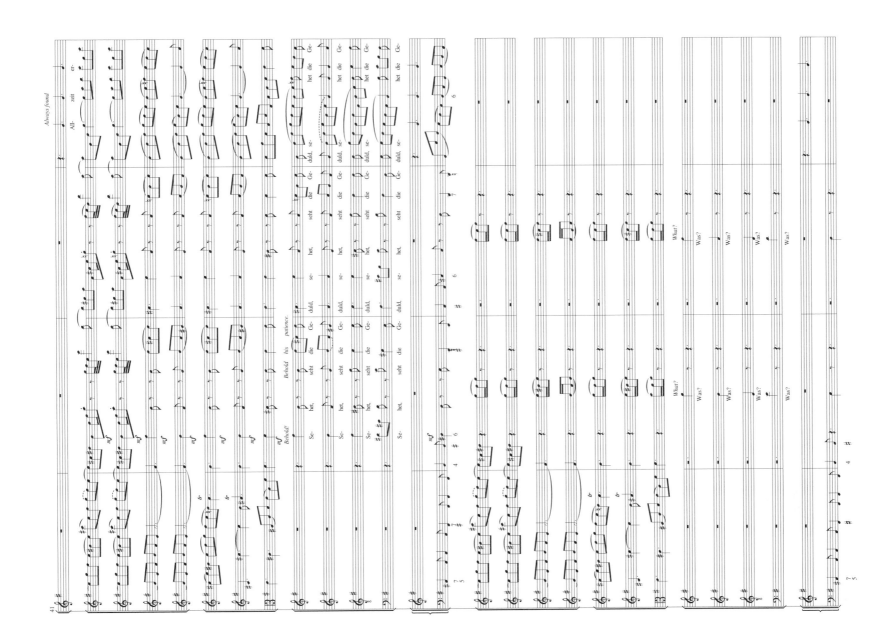

45
patient,
fund'n ge- dul- dig
although you were
Wie- wohl du
What?
Was?
Was?
Was?
Was?

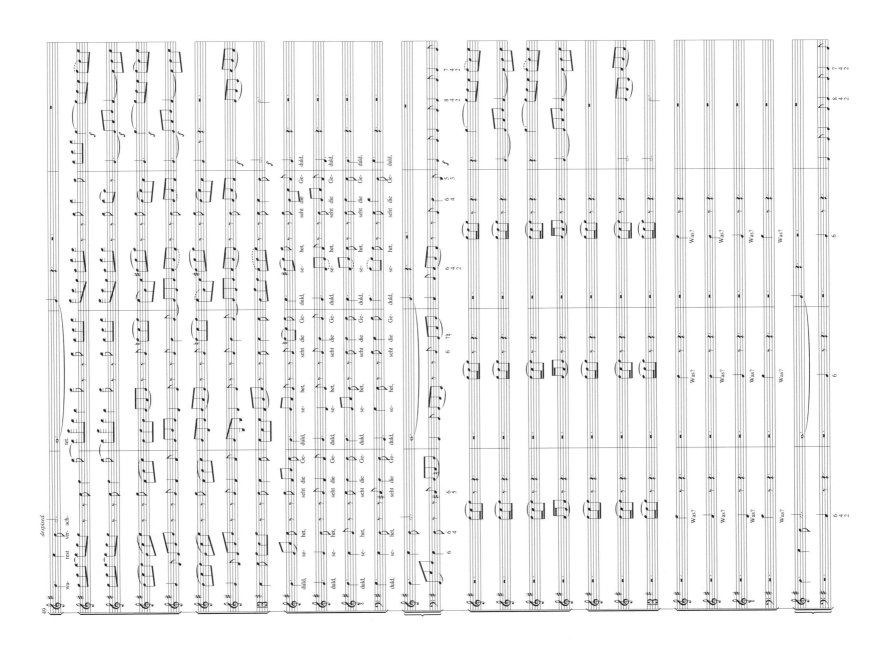

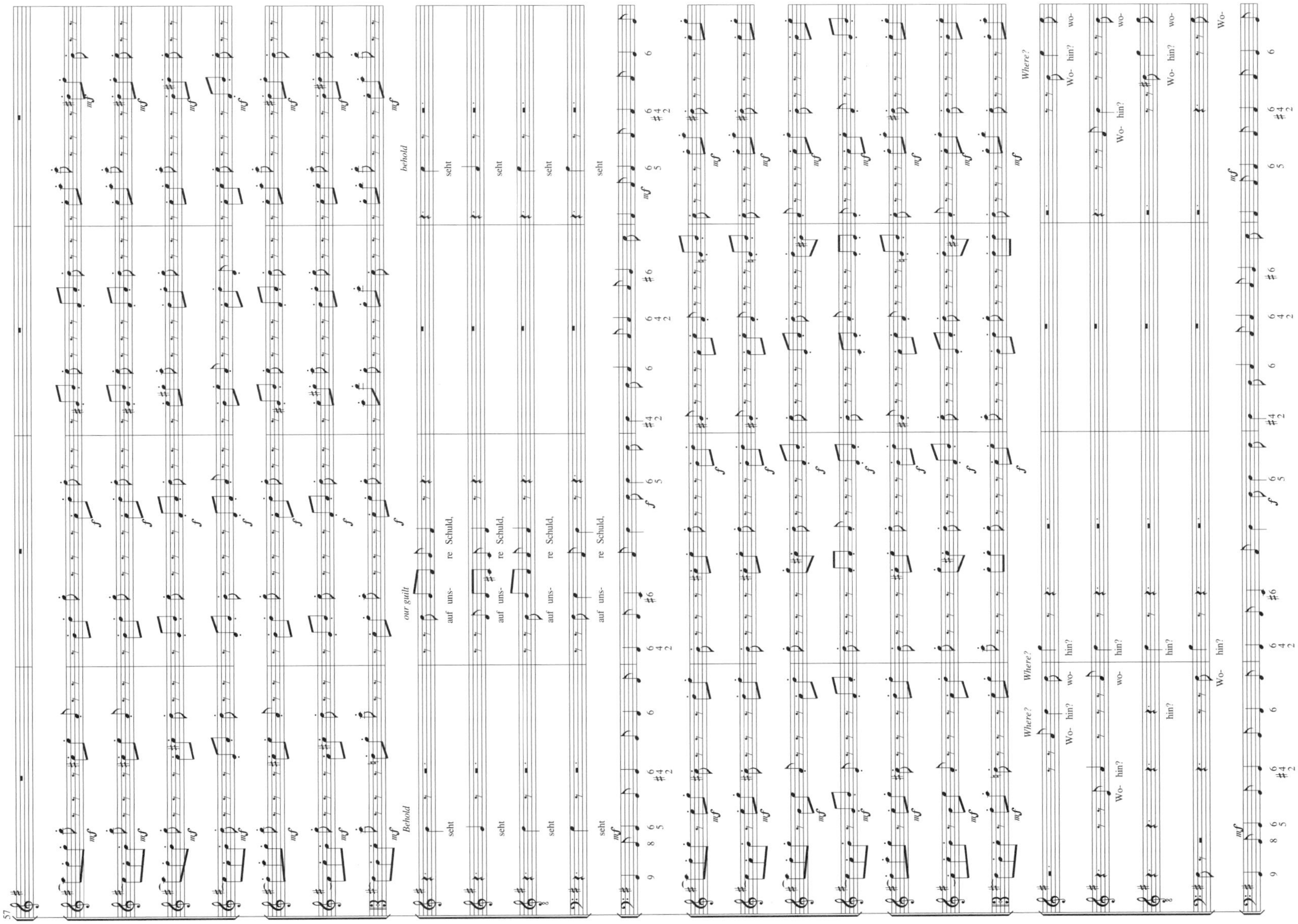
Behold
seht
our guilt
auf uns- re Schuld,
behold
Where?
Wo- hin?
wo-

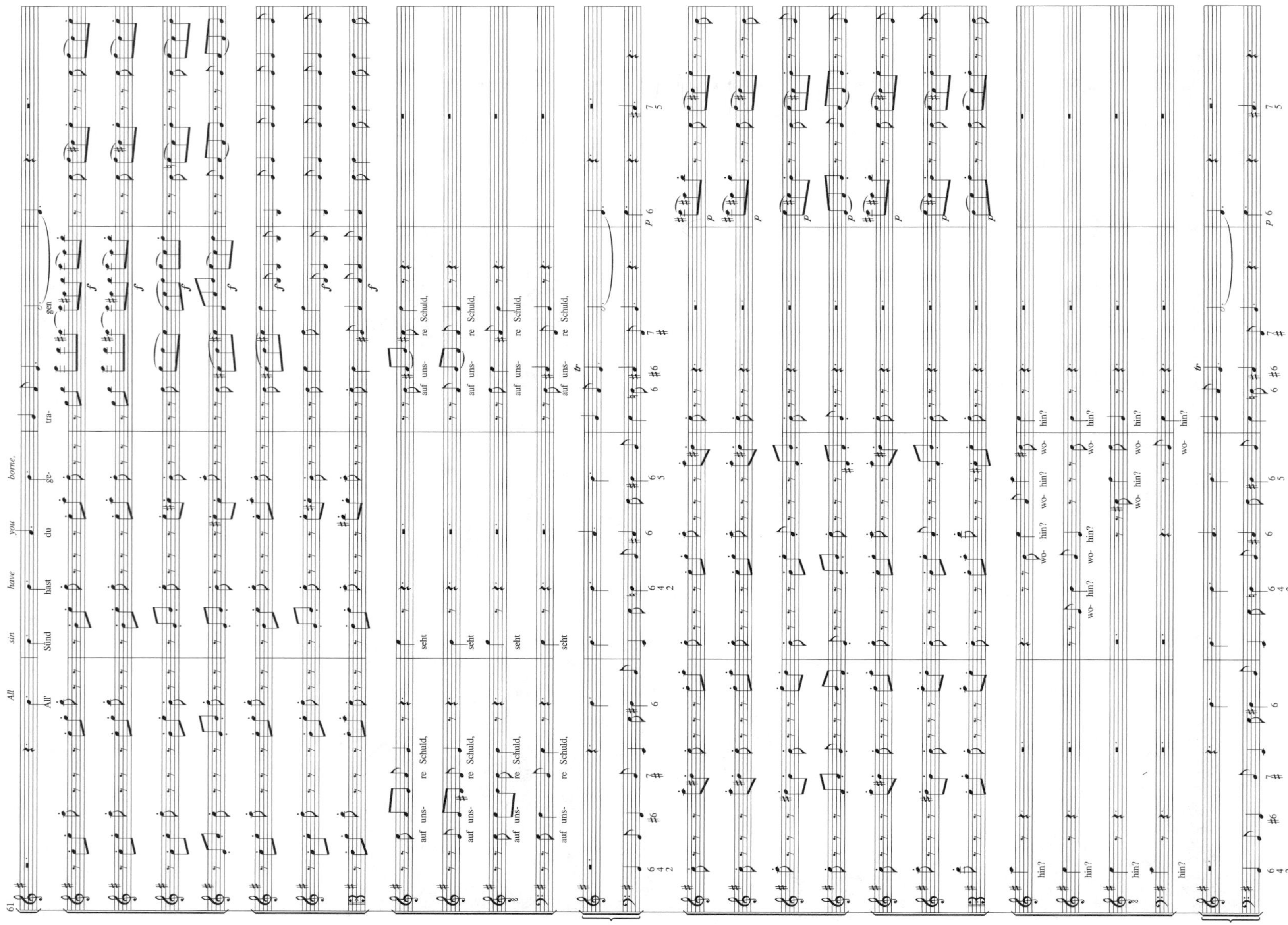
All sin have you borne,
All' Sünd hast du ge- tra- gen
auf uns- re Schuld, seht auf uns- re Schuld,
hin? wo- hin? wo- hin? wo- hin?

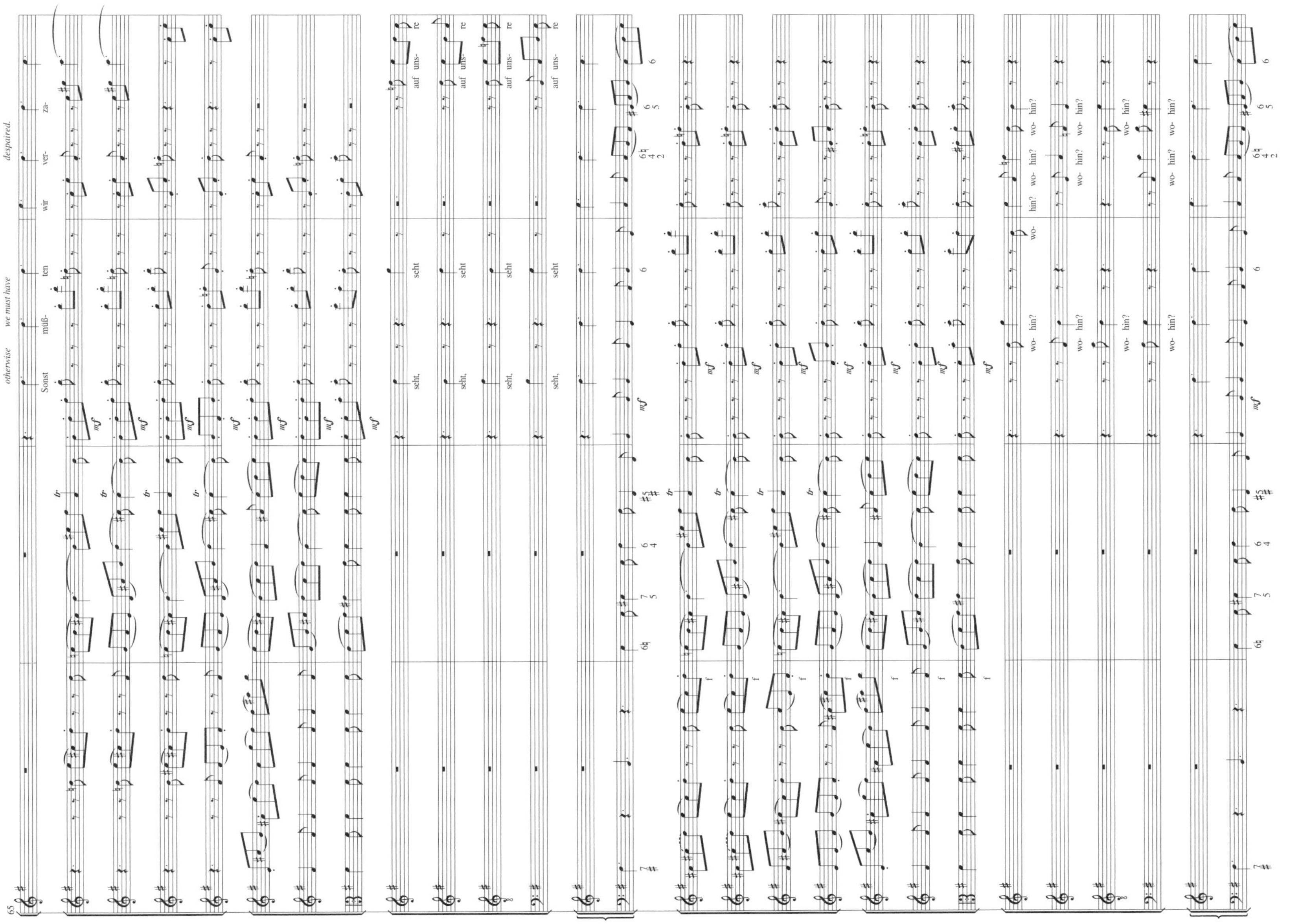
65
otherwise we must have despaired.
Sonst müß- ten wir ver- za-
seht, seht, auf uns- re
wo- hin? wo- hin? wo- hin?

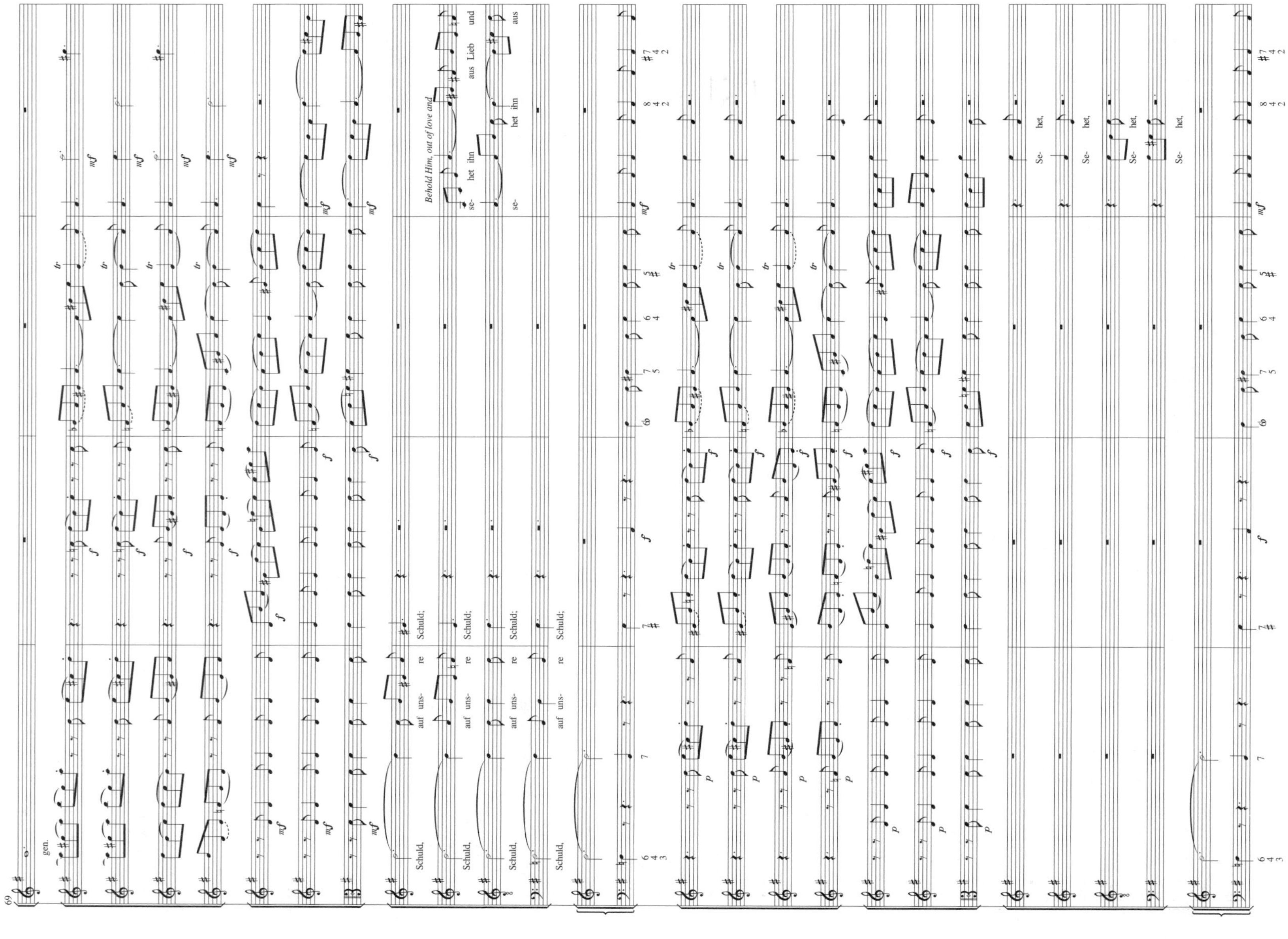
69
gen.
Schuld, auf uns- re Schuld;
Behold Him, out of love and
se- het ihn aus Lieb und
se- het ihn aus
Se- het,

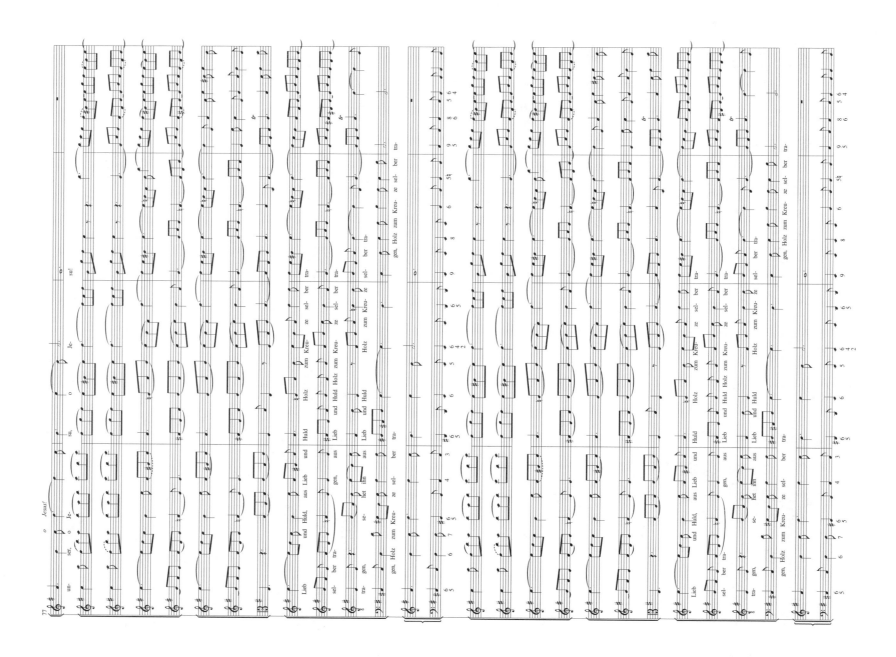

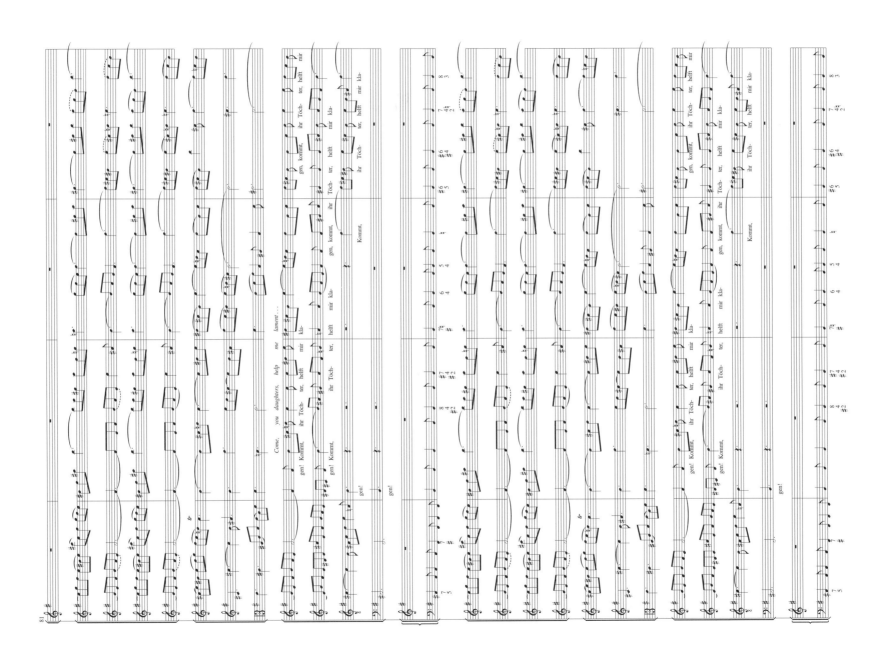

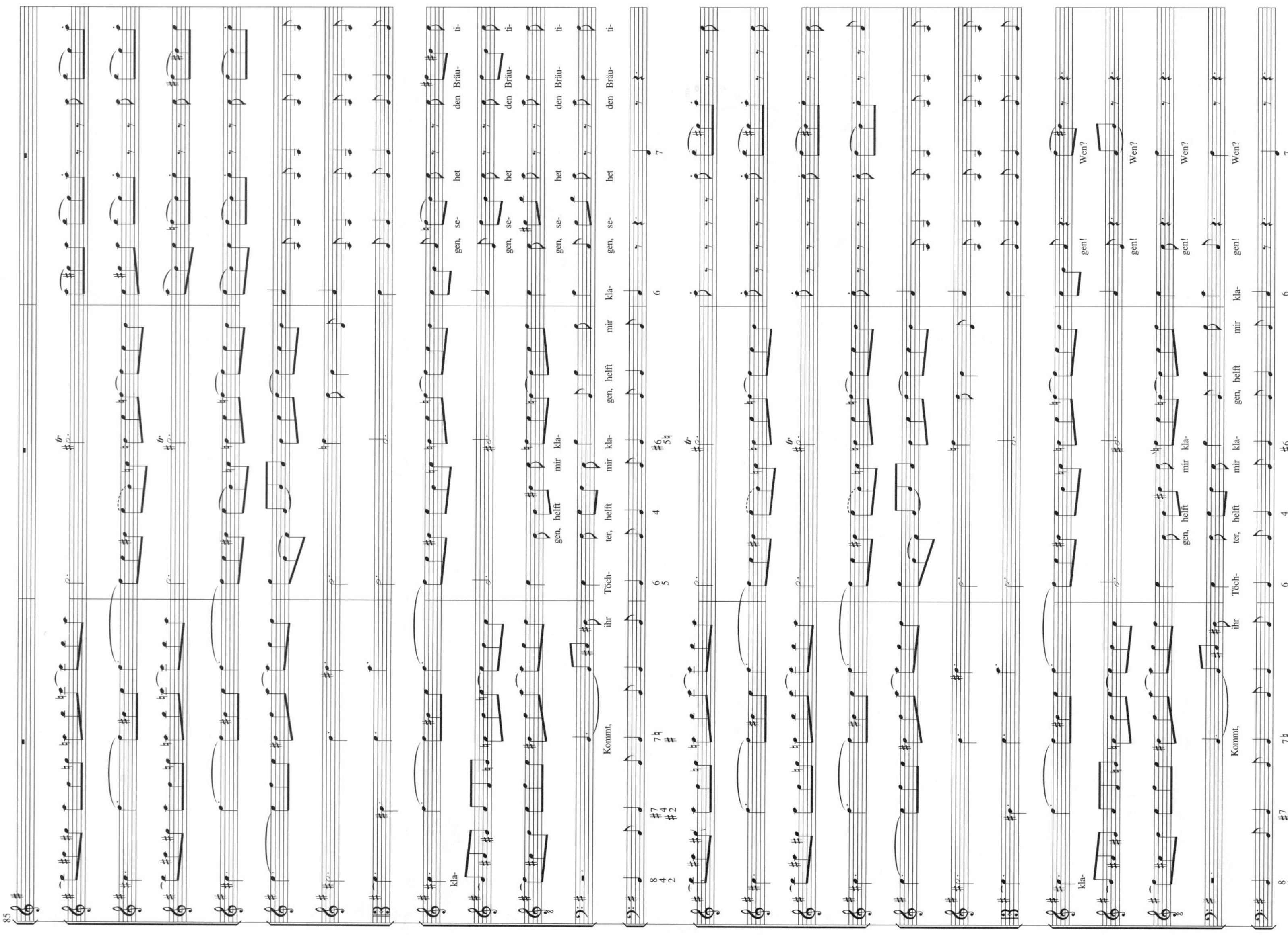
85
kla- gen, se- het den Bräu- ti-
gen, se- het den Bräu- ti-
gen, helft mir kla- gen, se- het den Bräu- ti-
Kommt, ihr Töch- ter, helft mir kla- gen, helft mir kla- gen, se- het den Bräu- ti-
kla- gen! Wen?
gen! Wen?
gen, helft mir kla- gen! Wen?
Kommt, ihr Töch- ter, helft mir kla- gen, helft mir kla- gen! Wen?

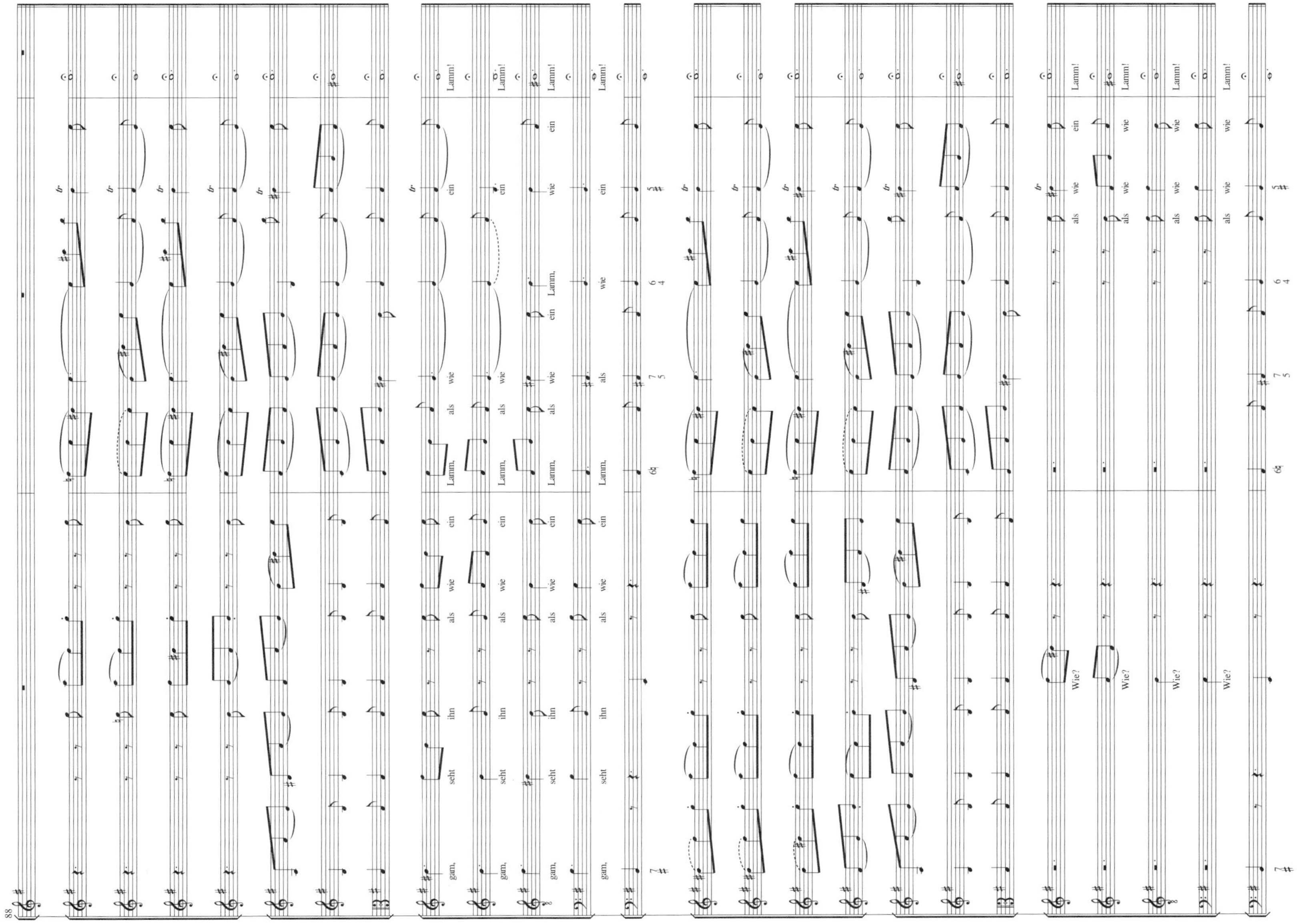
88
gan, seht ihn als wie ein Lamm, als wie ein Lamm!
gan, seht ihn als wie ein Lamm, als wie ein Lamm!
gan, seht ihn als wie ein Lamm, als wie ein Lamm, ein wie Lamm!
gan, seht ihn als wie ein Lamm, als wie Lamm!
Wie? als wie ein Lamm!
Wie? als wie wie Lamm!
Wie? als wie wie Lamm!
Wie? als wie wie Lamm!

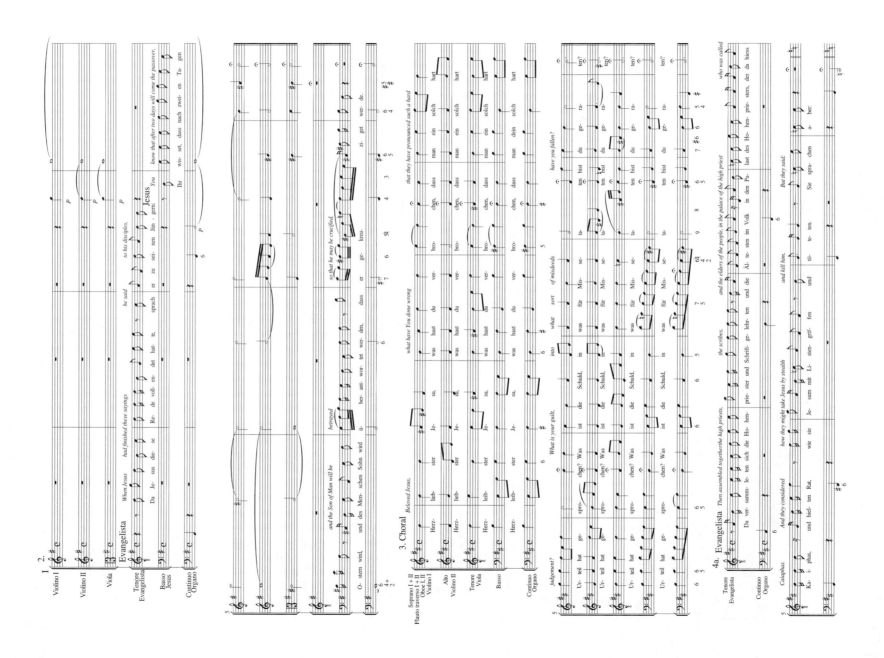

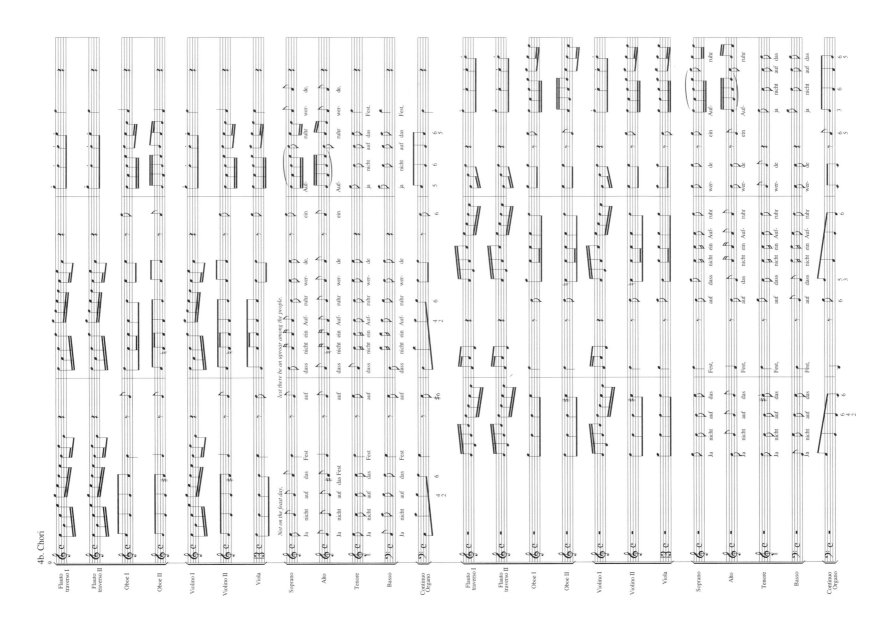

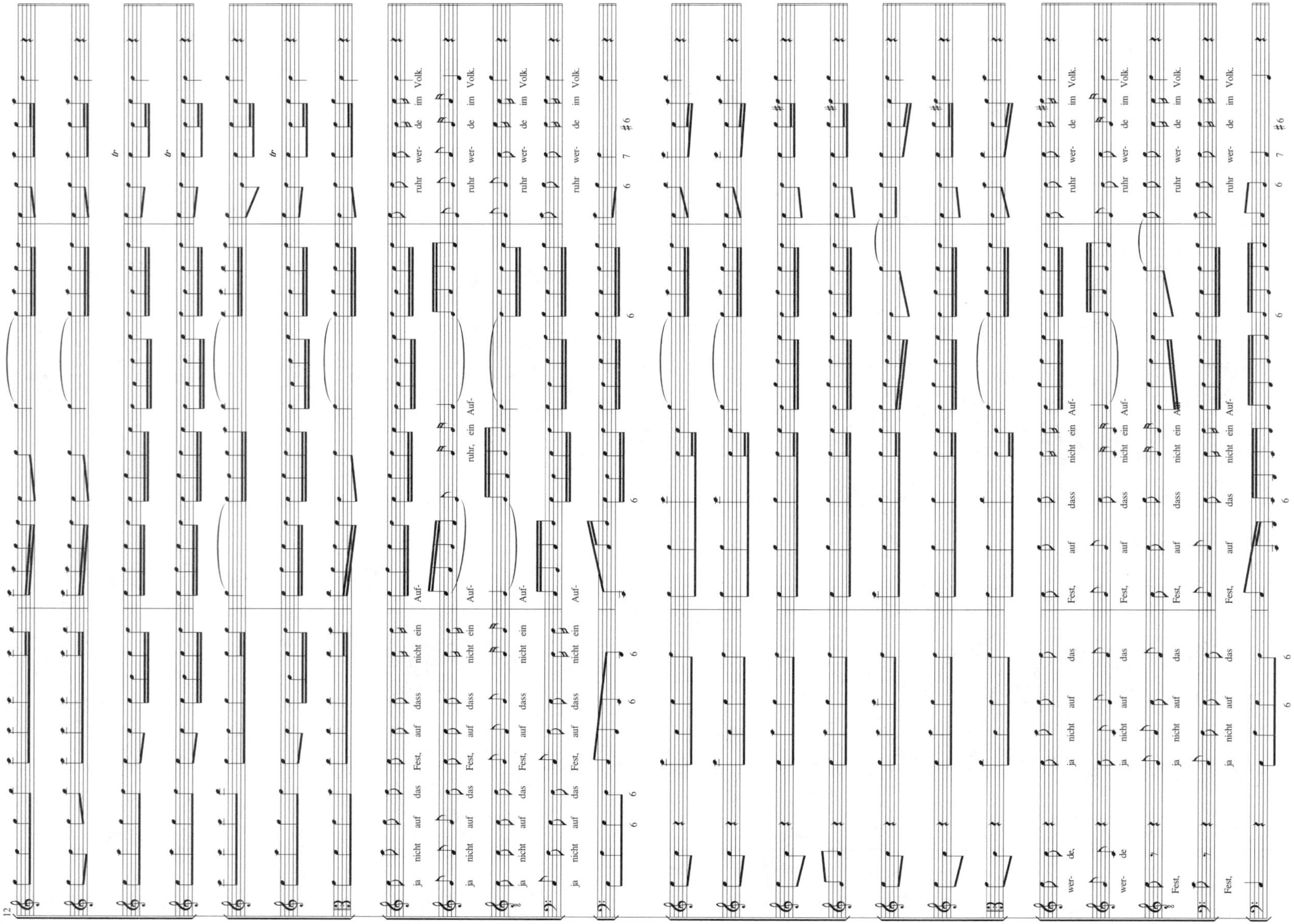
12
ja nicht auf das Fest, auf dass nicht ein Auf- ruhr wer- de im Volk.
ja nicht auf das Fest, auf dass nicht ein Auf- ruhr, ein Auf- ruhr wer- de im Volk.
wer- de, ja nicht auf das Fest, auf dass nicht ein Auf- ruhr wer- de im Volk.
Fest, ja nicht auf das Fest, auf dass nicht ein Auf- ruhr wer- de im Volk.

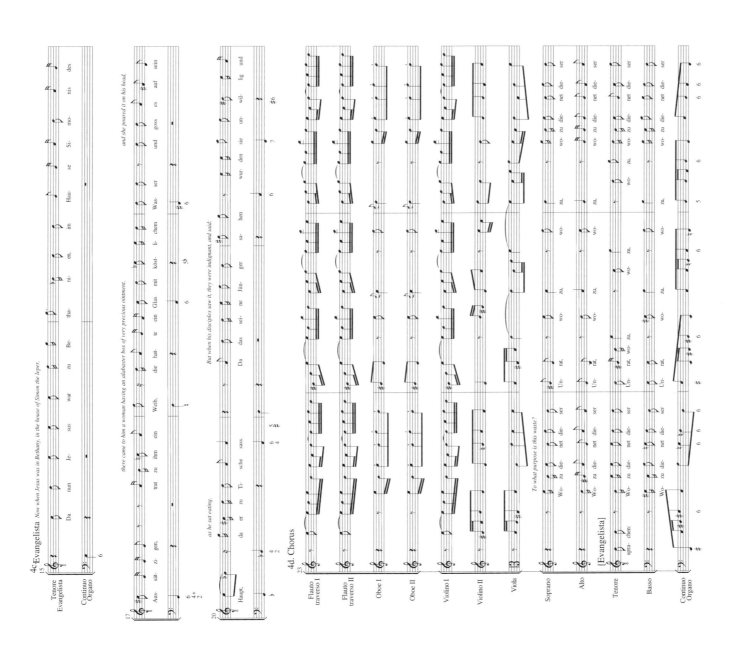

4c Evangelista *Now when Jesus was in Bethany, in the house of Simon the leper,*

there came to him a woman having an alabaster box of very precious ointment,

and she poured it on his head.

as he sat eating.

But when his disciples saw it, they were indignant, and said:

4d. Chorus

To what purpose is this waste?

[Evangelista]

For this ointment might have been sold for much and given to the poor.

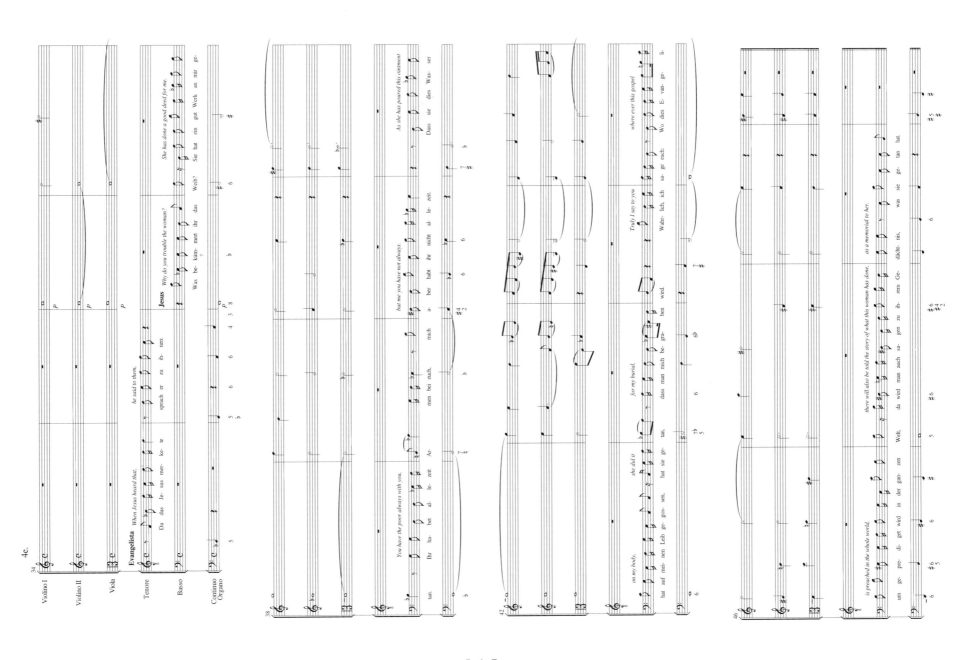

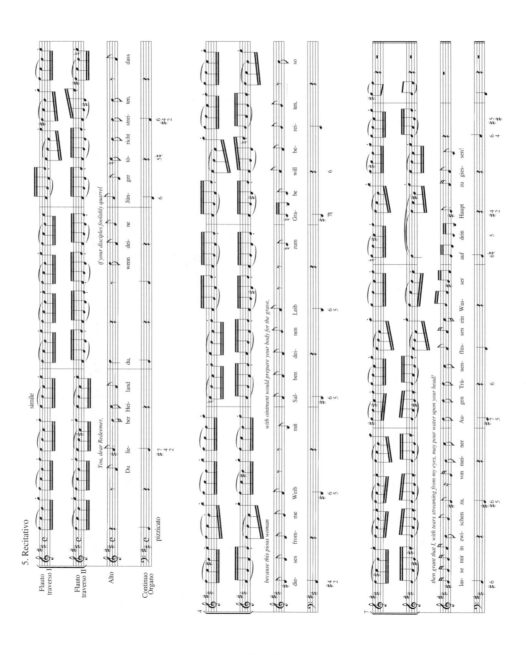

1. Chorus I & II:
Kommt, ihr Töchter, helft mir klagen...
Sehet!
Wen?
den Bräutigam. Sehet ihn
Wie?
als wie ein Lamm.

Choral:
O Lamm Gottes unschuldig
Am Stamm des Kreuzes geschlachtet

Chorus I & II:
Sehet!
Was?
Seht die Geduld.

Choral:
Allzeit erfund'n geduldig
Wiewohl du wärest verachtet.

Chorus I & II:
Seht...
Wohin?
auf unsre Schuld;

Choral:
All' Sünd hast du getragen,
Sonst müßten wir verzagen.

Chorus I & II:
Sehet ihn aus Lieb und Huld
Holz zum Kreuze selber tragen.

Choral:
Erbarm dich unser o Jesu!

2. Recitative
Evangelista:
Da Jesus diese Rede vollendet hatte, sprach er zu
seinen Jüngern:

Jesus:
Ihr wisset, daß nach zweien Tagen Ostern wird, und
des Menschen Sohn wird überantwortet werden, daß
er gekreuziget werde.

---

1. Chorus I & II:
Come, you daughters, help me lament...
See Him!
Whom?
The Bridegroom, behold Him!
How?
Like a Lamb.

Chorale:
O lamb of God inculpable
on the trunk of the cross slaughtered

Chorus I & II:
Behold!
What?
Behold His patience.

Chorale:
Always found patient,
although you were despised.

Chorus I & II:
Behold?
Where?
our guilt.

Chorale:
All sin have you borne,
otherwise we must have despaired.

Chorus I & II
Behold Him, out of love and grace,
the wood of the cross himself carrying.

Chorale:
Have mercy upon us, oh Jesus.

2. Recitative
Evangelist:
When Jesus had finished these sayings, he said to
his disciples:

Jesus:
You know that after two days will come the passover,
and the son of Man will be betrayed so that he may
be crucified

---

3. Choral:
Herzliebster Jesu, was hast du verbrochen,
Daß man ein solch hart Urteil hat gesprochen?
Was ist die Schuld? In was für Missetaten bist du
geraten?

4. Recitative
Evangelista:
Da versammleten sich die Hohenpriester und
Schriftgelehrten und die Ältesten im Volk in dem
Palast des Hohenpriesters, der da hieß Kaiphas. Und
hielten Rat, wie sie Jesum mit Listen griffen und
töteten. Sie sprachen aber:

Chorus I & II:
Ja nicht auf dieses Fest, auf daß nicht ein Aufruhr
werde im Volk.

Evangelista:
Da nun Jesus war zu Bethanien, im Hause Simonis,
des Aussätzigen, trat zu ihm ein Weib, das hatte ein
Glas mit köstlichem Wasser, und goß es auf sein
Haupt, da er zu Tische saß. Da das seine Jünger sahen,
wurden sie unwillig und sprachen:

Chorus I:
Wozu dienet dieser Unrat? Dieses Wasser hätte
mögen teuer verkauft und den Armen gegeben
werden.

Evangelista:
Da das Jesus merkete, sprach er zu ihnen:

Jesus:
Was bekümmert ihr das Weib? Sie hat ein gut Werk
an mir getan. Ihr habet allezeit Armen bei euch, mich
aber habt ihr nicht allezeit. Daß sie dies Wasser auf
meinen Leib gegossen, hat sie getan, daß man mich
begraben wird. Wahrlich, ich sage euch: Wo dies
Evangelium geprediget wird in der ganzen Welt, da
wird man auch sagen zu ihrem Gedächtnis, was sie
getan hat.

---

3. Chorale:
Beloved Jesus, what have you done wrong that they
have pronounced such a hard judgement? What is
your guilt, into what sort of misdeeds have your
fallen?

4. Recitative
Evangelist:
Then assembled together the chief priests, the
scribes, and the elders of the people, in the palace of
the high priest, who was called Caiaphas. And they
considered how they might take Jesus by stealth and
kill him. But they said,

Chorus I & II
Not on the feast day, lest there be an uproar among
the people.

Evangelist:
Now when Jesus was in Bethany, in the house of
Simon the leper, there came to him a woman having
an alabaster box of very precious ointment, and she
poured it on his head, as he sat eating. But when his
disciples saw it, they were indignant and said:

Chorus I:
To what purpose is this waste? For this ointment
might have been sold for much and given to the
poor.

Evangelist:
When Jesus heard that, he said to them,

Jesus:
Why do you trouble the woman? She has done a
good deed for me. The poor you have always with
you, but me you have not always. As she has poured
this oinment on my body, she did it for my burial.
Truly I say to you, wherever this gospel is preached
in the whole world, there will also be told the
story of what this woman has done, as a memorial
to her.

5. Recitativo:
Du lieber Heiland du,
Wenn deine Jünger töricht streiten,
Daß dieses fromme Weib
Mit Salben deinen Leib
Zum Grabe will bereiten,
So lasse mir inzwischen zu,
Von meiner Augen Tränenflüssen
Ein Wasser auf dein Haupt zu gießen.

6. Aria:
Buß und Reu
Knirscht das Sündenherz entzwei,
Daß die Tropfen meiner Zähren
Angenehme Spezerei,
Treuer Jesu, dir gebären.
   Buß und Reu...

5. Recitative:
You, dear Redeemer,
if your disciples foolishly quarrel
because this pious woman
with ointment would prepare your body
for the grave,
then grant that I,
with tear streaming from my eyes,
may pour water upon your head!

6. Aria:
Penance and remorse
tear the sinful heart in two.
May the drops of my tears
be an acceptable anointing
to you, faithful Jesus.
   Penance and remorse..

127 JOHANN SEBASTIAN BACH, Passacaglia and Fugue, BWV 582 (ca. 1707)

from D:Bsb, Mus. ms. Bach P 803

Thema fugatum

128a Chorale "Allein Gott in der Höh sei Ehr"

Allein Gott in der Höh sei Ehr
Und Dank für seine Gnade,
Darum, daß nun und nimmermehr
Uns rühren kann kein Schade.
Ein Wohlgefallen Gott an uns hat;
Nun ist gross Fried ohn Unterlaß,
All Fehd hat uns ein Ende.

God alone in the highest be praised
and be thanked for His Grace,
by which now and evermore
we can rest without harm.
A blessing God has given us;
now there is peace without end,
all strife has ended for us.

128b JOHANN SEBASTIAN BACH, *Allein Gott in her Höh sei Ehr*, BWV 663
(ca. 1708–17, revised ca. 1749),

from D:Bsb, Mus. ms. Bach P 271

129 JOHANN SEBASTIAN BACH, Praeludium 21 and Fuga 21 à 3 (1722)

from *Das Wohltemperirte Clavier*, Vol. 1, D:Bsb,

Mus. ms. Bach P415

130 JOHANN SEBASTIAN BACH, Concerto 1ᵐᵒ from *Six Concerts Avec plusieurs Instruments* (Brandenburg Concerto no. 1, ?1713/?1716/1721), BWV 1046,

from D:Bsb, am. B. 78

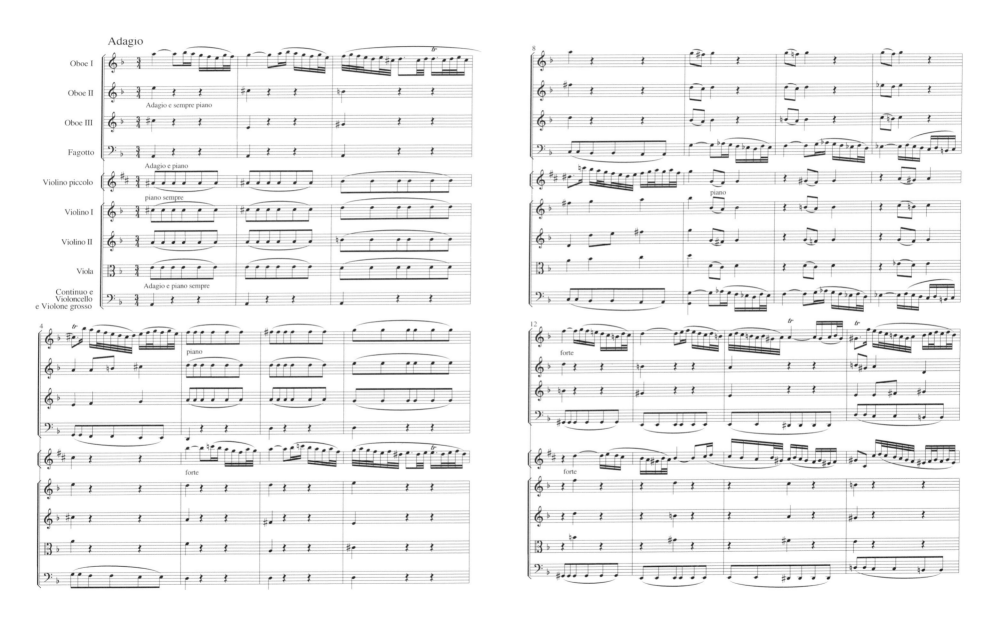

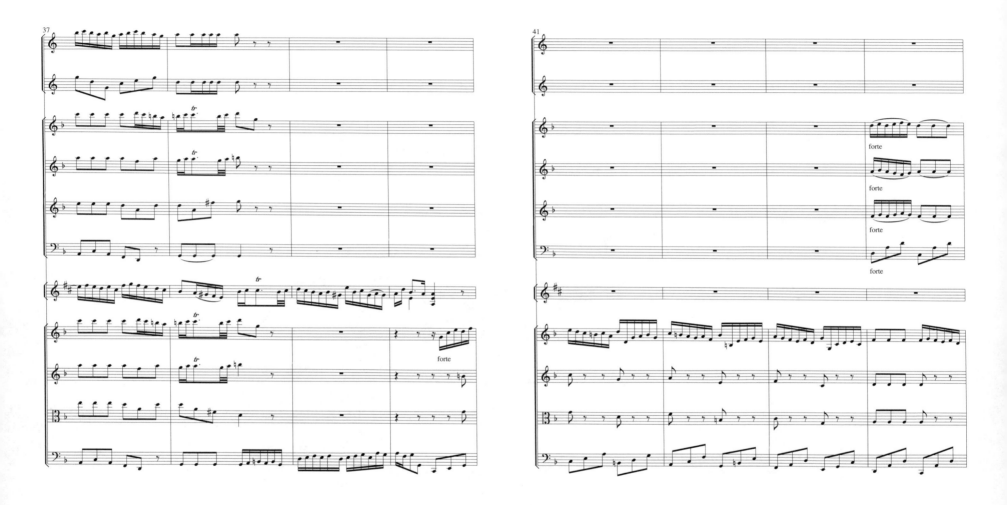

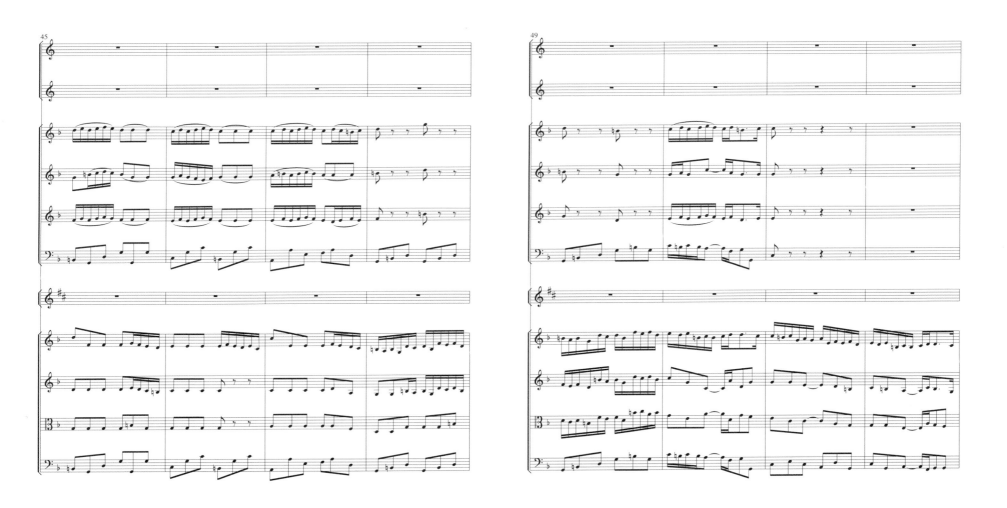

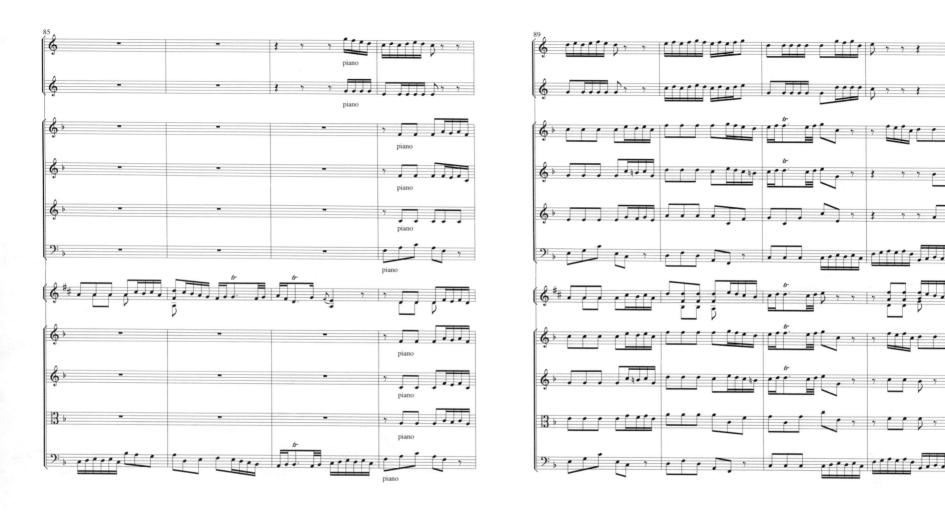

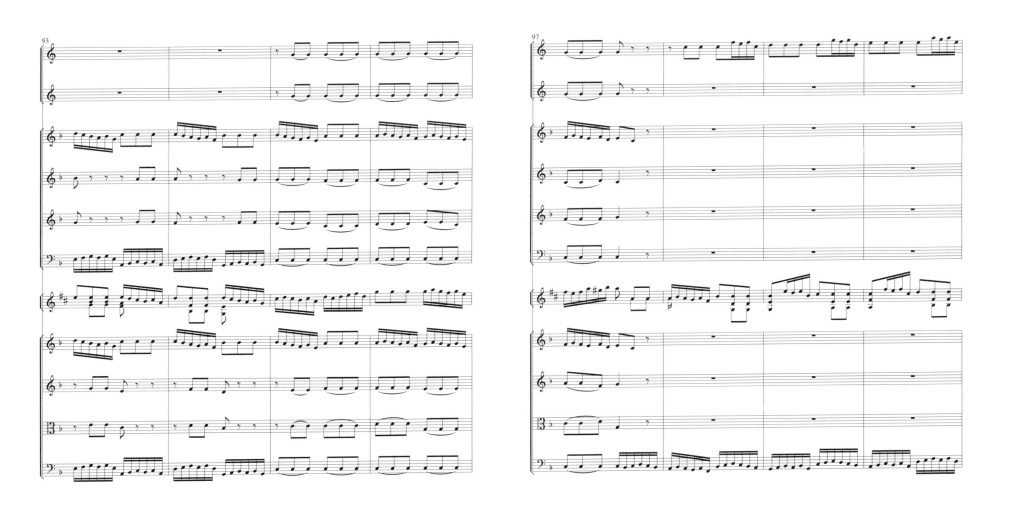

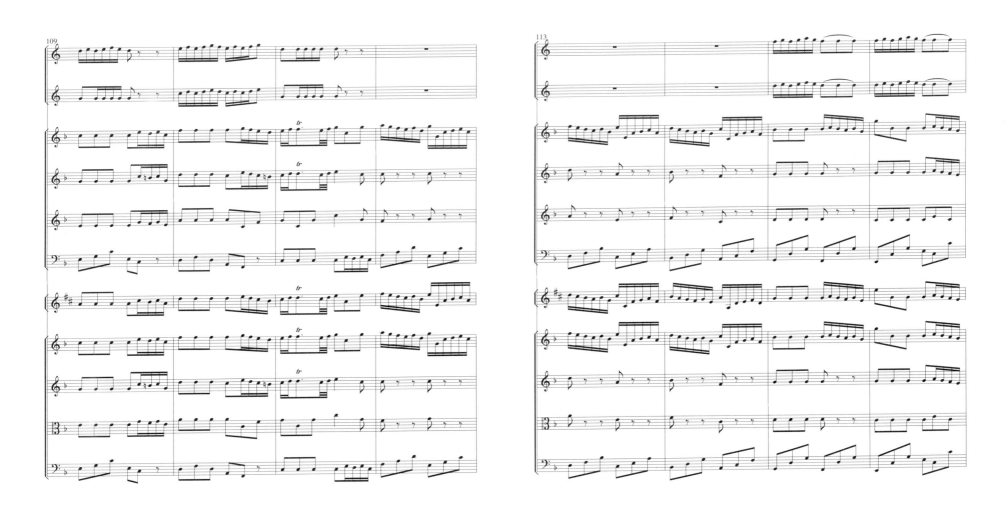

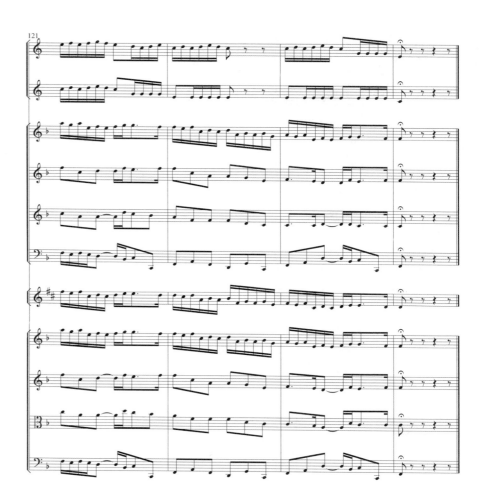

Menuetto

Trio

Oboe I

Oboe II

Fagotto

Polacca

Menuetto da Capo, e poi la Polacca.

Violino I

piano

Violino II

piano

Viola

piano

Continuo
e Violoncello
e Violone grosso

piano

Menuetto da Capo, e poi il Trio.

Trio

Corno I

Corno II

Tutte le Oboi

Menuetto da Capo sino alla Fine.